CROSS-CULTURAL LEADERSHIP

Ministering to a Multicultural Community

By

Louis M. Ao and David R. Penley

CROSS-CULTURAL LEADERSHIP
by Louis M. Ao and David R. Penley

Printed in the United States of America

ISBN 1-60034-590-5

www.xulonpress.com

Brother Rick,

My God richly bless you wonderful ministry.

Louis A.

Dedication

From Louis:
> This book is dedicated to my lovely wife Aienla and to my dear children Rachel and Tia Akum Ao.

From David:
> This book is lovingly dedicated to my parents Harvey and Barbara Penley, who taught me by word and action to love all people as God loves them – unconditionally, and to my wife, Sabra, and children, Elyse and Philip, who show me unconditional love and gave me the time to help write this book.

TABLE OF CONTENTS

FORWARD xi

INTRODUCTION xiii

1. **THE NEED FOR CROSS-CULTURAL MINISTRY** 21
   Introduction 21
   The Changing American Landscape 22
   A Biblical/Theological Rationale 27
   Conclusion 59

2. **FOUNDATIONAL TRUTHS FOR MULTICULTURAL MINISTRY** 63
   Introduction 63
   Cross-Cultural Ministry Requires Being
      Biblical 64
   Cross-Cultural Ministry Requires
      Commitment 66
   Cross-Cultural Ministry Requires
      Patience 70

Cross-Cultural Ministry Requires
Prayer 83
Cross-Cultural Ministry Requires
Humility 87
Cross-Cultural Ministry Requires
Discernment 93
Conclusion 95

3. **PRACTICING CROSS-CULTURAL MINISTRY: RESEARCHING YOUR COMMUNITY** **97**
Introduction...97
Know Your Community 102
What We Want to Learn 124
Conclusion 140

4. **PRACTICING CROSS-CULTURAL MINISTRY: TURNING RESEARCH INTO RESULTS**.....................................**141**
Introduction...141
Preparing a Church to Be
Cross-Cultural 142
Cross-Cultural Ministry and
Transformational Leadership
Strategies...151
Cross-Cultural Conflict Resolution..........173
Sharing the Gospel Cross-Culturally 180
Ministry to International Students:
An Example of Cross-Cultural
Ministry...184
Conclusion 191

CONCLUSION 195

APPENDIX

   1. **WEEKLY TRAINING PLAN**...............199
   2. **RETREAT PLAN**....................................207
   3. **CROSS-CULTURAL/**
      MULTICULTURAL MINISTRY
      WORKSHEET...213
   4. **FOUNDATIONAL TRUTHS FOR**
      MULTICULTURAL MINISTRY
      WORKSHEET...215
   5. **UNDERSTANDING OTHER**
      CULTURES WORKSHEET.................217
   6. **DISCUSSION GUIDE FOR**
      UNDERSTANDING OTHER
      CULTURES WORKSHEET.................219
   7. **RESEARCHING OUR**
      COMMUNITY.......................................223
   8. **COMMUNITY MEMBER**
      QUESTIONNAIRE................................225

BIBLIOGRAPHY..227

FORWARD

The Great Commission given to the church by the Great Commissioner is clear and precise; we are to make disciples of everybody, everywhere teaching them everything that Christ taught His disciples. While the assignment is clear the implementation can be quite challenging in the culturally and ethnically diverse environment of urban society.

Dr. Louis Ao and Dr. David Penley, pastors, professors, disciplers and researchers have provided timely insight and valuable advice for those commissioned to fulfill the Commission in the urban context. Their able and thorough research coupled with their keen and accurate theological perspective have combined to produce a handbook that will prove to be a vital tool for those ministering in the multi-cultural context. I hope that you will take the time to work through the detail of their findings and prayerfully apply the principles that they have mined through their meticulous research.

Reverend Gary L. Frost
Executive Director
Metropolitan New York Baptist Association
New York City

INTRODUCTION

America is a land of diversity in culture. From the country's beginning, its early settlers had to deal with cultural diversity and ministry issues. When the thirteen colonies developed along the East Coast of America, the so-called "Western Civilization" was a mixture of much diversity; for example, the Puritans were in Massachusetts and did not allow Roger Williams to build a Baptist chapel in their territory. He had to go to Rhode Island. Lord Baltimore secured permission from the British Crown to establish Maryland as a safe haven for Catholics. William Penn created a state where Quakers were welcomed. In Virginia, the state church was Anglican. This is diversity aplenty (Belgum, 177-81).

We can conclude from these facts that cultural diversity is certainly not a new scenario on American soil. The late United States President, John F. Kennedy, called the United States "a nation of immigrants" (Pocock and Henriques, 16). The first settlers in America were the Native Americans who came here thousands of years ago as immigrants from Asia

(Encyclopedia Britannica, 15th ed., s.v., "American Indians"). Today America is more diverse than ever (Rhodes, 15).

This book deals with critical ministry issues that arise for the local church because of this cultural diversity in America. We will look at the need for cross-cultural ministry based on both the practical realities of the changes occurring in the United States population and the clear teachings of God's Word. We will then look at some of the implications for ministry that come from these needs. Finally, we will present ideas about how to do ministry in an increasing multicultural society. Before we do any of that, however, it is important that we define some key terms used in this book.

The Definitions of Culture

To understand cross-cultural ministry, the word culture needs to be defined. Webster's Dictionary defines it as: "the totality of socially transmitted behavior patterns, arts, beliefs, institutions, and all other products of human work and thought typical of a population or community at a given time" (Webster's II New College Dictionary 1999, s.v. "culture")" Shorter describes culture as follows:

Culture is a comprehensive concept, which embraces all that individuals acquire or learn as members of a human society. One of the functions of culture is to help people relate cognitively, affectively and behaviorally to experience. Culture offers a pattern of meanings embodied in images or symbols. These control the individual's perception of reality. Culture also results in the creation of a group identity and of adaptive strategy for living and surviving (Shorter, 30).

Other experts define the comprehensive nature of culture. Marvin K. Mayers states that:

Culture is everything that is a part of one's everyday life experience. It includes: tangibles such as food, shelter, clothing, literature, art, music, etc.; and intangibles such as hopes, dreams, values, rules, space, relationships, language, body movements, etc. (Mayers, xi).

Donald K. Smith writes:

The core of a culture is not a miscellaneous collection of beliefs and values. Instead, it provides a large consistent interpretation of life (Smith, 260).

Patty Lane writes that culture can be understood at two different levels. One level is the objective. These are the above surface aspects that are obvious to everyone. These include such things as food, clothing, time consciousness, whether or not eye contact is made, and how one greets another. These aspects can be adapted fairly quickly to function easily in the predominant American culture when a person comes to live here. The second level is the subjective. It is below the surface. It remains, even if the outward appearances change. This is the inner motivation of the person; the inner beliefs and world-view. It includes such aspects as beliefs about gender and authority roles, concepts of the truth, and other basic values. These change much more slowly and some never do. Thus it is important that we understand a culture from both aspects if the church is to effectively minister to persons from that culture (Lane, 18-19).

The definitions above help us to understand the commonalities that exist among all mankind. They also help us to realize that God has created us with differences. It is critical that the church thinks through and learns about how all cultures have similar needs and how God would have the church take part in meeting those needs, while seeking to do so in a way that best relates to a particular culture.

Cross-Cultural and Multicultural Ministry

Two other concepts must be understood for the purpose of this book. One is multicultural ministry. This refers to a church or ministry that is influenced by several cultures, but has no predominant or prevalent culture (Romo, 49). While this term has come to be used to include many different dimensions including age, gender, sexual preference, and regional differences (Yancey, 18), we will use the term to refer to churches and ministries that seek to reach out to all persons regardless of their culture. Charles Lyons, pastor of the multicultural Armitage Baptist Church in Chicago states the following about multicultural ministry in the process of describing the growth of his church:

> Our first tactic was simply to get to people. We had no mission statement, but we had a mission: reach anybody you can, anywhere you can. Multicultural ministry is not about methods. It is first about people. Keep talking with people in a multicultural setting and you will eventually penetrate other cultures. The differences may be race or language, or geographic or economic (Lyons, 49).

Multiculturalism is therefore in sharp contrast to cultural assimilation which assumes the dominance of one group over another. It assumes instead that that no one culture stands over another (Ruffle, 74-5); no culture is perfect, but every culture has value. Multiethnic and multiracial are other terms that are also used for this type of church or ministry, but we will use multicultural.

A second important term in this book is cross-cultural. This refers to churches that desire to reach out to people of all backgrounds, including those that are different from the culture that makes up the largest number of members of the congregation. These churches are not only open to other cultures, but they make changes that allow them to demonstrate that they value all cultures and thus makes them more likely to reach persons of other cultures.

If a church desires to be multicultural – to reach all persons of all backgrounds in its community – then it must be purposely cross-cultural. And if a church desires to truly be effective in America today, it must be willing to reach out cross-culturally. As one seminary vice-president, Rodrick Durst stated:

> Real world ministry in urban and suburban contexts means intercultural ministry. No church leader can be effective today without serious training in the understanding, penetration, and assimilation of different cultures and generations into one congregation. ("Golden Gate," 2)

We will spend the rest of this book discussing how to do this. We will begin in the first chapter by trying to motivate you to be committed to multicultural ministry by demonstrating the practical need for it, and by showing the biblical mandate for it. In chapter two, we will show some basic truths about multicultural ministry that you must accept if you are to be effective at it. We will discuss in the third chapter how to research a community so that you can discover who lives there. Finally in chapter four, we will suggest some practical methods that will help a church be cross-cultural so that it can become multicultural, as well as how to respond to some specific issues that may arise as a church seeks to practice cross-cultural ministry. We also will provide some ideas for introducing the concepts in this book to others in your church. It is our prayer that this book will challenge you and then will provide some guidance for you to reach out to the ever changing community that your church ministers to.

CHAPTER 1

THE NEED FOR CROSS-CULTURAL MINISTRY

Introduction

The need for Christians to communicate across cultures has always been a biblical fact, but the Church in America has recently developed a stronger and clearer recognition of this scriptural mandate. Based on the teaching of the Bible found in such passages as Matthew 28:19, where Christians are called to "go and make disciples of all nations," the Church has prayed for the salvation of lost persons of all nationalities. Until recently, that prayer has been fulfilled by the American Church sending missionaries who are called to go to other countries. Then America began to change. God has been in the process of answering our prayers by sending the nations to us. Reaching out to people of other nationalities is no longer only for those Christians called to go overseas. It is now for those Christians who have been called to take the Gospel message to their neighbors. This means all believers. This chapter will make a case that it is an absolute necessity that the Church in the United States be willing to learn how to effectively minister across cultures. It will be shown that the need is there because of the changing demographic landscape of America, but it is even more a need if the Church desires to be faithful to the teachings of God's Word.

The Changing American Landscape

The need for the Church to be involved in cross-cultural ministry is clearly seen in the changes that have taken place in the demographic makeup of America. This change has been experienced directly by the writers of this book. As I (David) co-write this chapter, my neighbors who live in the houses directly around me are Vietnamese, Mexican (first genera-tion immigrants), and African American. If I go up the block I will find Indians, Africans, Iranians, Burmese, Koreans, Thais, and Chinese among others. Since all of these people live in my neighborhood, they also live in my church's neighborhood. If the church is going to survive, much less prosper, grow, and carry out its mission to reach its community with the Gospel, it must come to grips with this changing environment and learn to minister across cultures.

This evidence observed by my own eyes is also seen in the demographic data that clearly shows what has been happening in the United States. The result of changing immigration laws and the migration of people to the United States in recent years is that we now look different as a nation. Rhodes States: "From 1980-1990, the United States experienced the largest amount of immigration since the turn of the century, as well as the most racially and ethnically diverse ever" (Rhodes, 121). Between 1960 and 1990, the foreign born population of the United States grew from 9.7 million to 19.7 million, a 103% increase. Cities have especially felt the impact in this growth of foreign born persons. Los Angeles (29.3%), San Francisco (28.3%), New York (22.8%), Dallas/Fort Worth (12.8%), Boston (12.5%), and Chicago (12.3%) are all examples of cities with a high percentage of their population born outside the United States according to the 2000 census (infoplease.com). Immigrants began to look more distinct and to compose large, distinct blocks of people, making the process of assimilation, widely assumed to be the goal of immigrants, more difficult (Salins, 39). According to Dixie L. Hunke: "Social scientists no longer call America a melting pot. America is a casserole or stew, with each ingredient retaining a distinctive flavor while subtly changing the taste of the whole dish" (Hunke, 2)

While the non-Hispanic white population grew between 1980 and 2004 (from 194 million to 235 million, a 17% increase), the non-white population increased from 46 million to 98 million, a 106% increase. The result has been a decrease in the non-Hispanic white population from 79.5% to 69% of the overall population, while the non-white population has increased from 20.5 to 31% of the overall population. This has especially been seen among Hispanics (from 6 to 14% of the total population), African Americans (from 12 to 13% of the total population), and Asians (from 1.5 to 4.5% of the total population) (Hunke, 2). This can all be summed up by the fact that in the United States during this period, the combined population of Hispanics, African Americans, and Asians, along with Native Americans and Pacific Islanders grew at 13 times the rate of non-Hispanic whites. If these trends continue, it is estimated that by the year 2050, half the population of the United States will be non-white (prb.org).

This type of growth among non-whites can best be seen in specific parts of the nation. More than half (51%) of the minority population lived in five states in 2004 (California, New York, Texas, Illinois, and Hawaii) (prb.org). In 2004, Texas joined California, New Mexico, and Hawaii as states where the total minority population outnumbers the majority Anglo population. While the Anglo population in these states still outnumbers any single minority group's population, the population of all other groups in those states has grown to outdistance them. Experts say this is a trend that will be seen nationwide in the future. One demographer states that "if anyone wants to see what the United States will look like for their children or grandchildren, they need to look at Texas now (dfw. com)." California has the largest population of both Hispanics (11 million or nearly one of every three Hispanics in the United States) and Asians (3.6

million), while New York has the largest population of African-Americans (2.8 million) (prb.org).

All of this has led many sociologists to conclude that the United States has transitioned to a truly multi-cultural nation (prb.org). This means that the church must respond to this multicultural society or face becoming irrelevant. Unfortunately, the church has not responded all that well. Manuel Ortiz, professor at Westminster Theological Seminary in Philadelphia, writes of becoming a Christian and realizing that "the life of the church was in most cases segregated, by design and by desire, on the basis of racism and ethnocentrism" (Ortiz, 15). Michael Pocock and Joseph Henriques indicate that:

> Many Christians and local churches have failed to 'do the right thing' in response to ethnic change. They have faithfully responded to Christ's Great Commission in Matthew 28:19-20, sending missionaries around the globe, but they have not always been so dili-gent or even friendly when the peoples of the world have come to their neighborhood. There are three obstacles to overcome by Anglo American churches, namely: Ethnocentrism, Nationalism, and Traditionalism. (Pocock and Henriques, 16)

Another place the need for cross-cultural ministry can be observed is on the campuses of colleges and universities in the United States. In the decade of the 1990's, the number of students from abroad coming to the United States increased at the rate of 12,000 per year. In 1964, the number of foreign nationals studying, teaching, or doing research work at U.S. institutions of higher education or training as interns or residents in American hospitals was 91,995. Thirty years later, in 1994, that number was 438,000. Today that number is over 500,000 (Thurber, 612).

In the mid-1960's, almost 35% of students came from Asia. Today, students from Asian nations still lead the way. China is first with 10.3% of all foreign students in the United States, or over 50,000 persons. Next on the list are Japan, 9.8%; India, 8.2%; Taiwan, 8.5%; the Republic of Korea, 6.5%. Canada, which led all countries in the mid-1960's, now is sixth on the list with 4.8%. California leads all states in receiving 13 % of all students who come to the United States. New York and Texas are next in line, Texas having risen from eighth place thirty years ago (Thurber, 613).

By bringing more than 500,000 international students to the United States from more than 200 countries and political areas, God has placed in our midst a tremendous privilege, responsibility, and opportunity for fulfilling the Great Commission. Add spouses and children to those 500,000 plus students, include those on government and business exchange programs, and that opportunity becomes even more dramatic – upwards of one million people. These are the world's most gifted and intelligent people. Rich in culture and fluent in several languages, they come with a desire to learn, to succeed educationally, and to contribute to society (Selle, 18). As Carl Selle states:

Without leaving our own land, or for that matter, our own community, we are given the chance to be world ambassadors for the Lord Jesus Christ. By exposing internationals to us, the Holy Spirit is shaping the attitudes of those destined to be prominent leaders who may one day be deciding the fate of Christian work in their countries. These international students will become prominent educators, parents, journalists, politicians, engineers, scientists, and jurists. (Selle, 18)

Thus for a very practical reason – to survive in the midst of a changing world – the Church must learn to reach across cultures. But there is an even more important reason the church must seek to bridge the cultural chasm – because God calls us to do so.

A Biblical/Theological Rationale

It is essential that a church's ministry flow out of the teachings of the Word of God. God through His Word teaches that ministering across cultures is to be a part of the work of the Church. Evidence of this is found in the life and teachings of Jesus. The disciples demonstrated that they understood their Lord's emphasis in their own teaching and writing. The early church grasped the concept and practiced cross-cultural ministry. Therefore, we will look first at the Gospels to discover what Jesus has to say about cross-cultural ministry. Then we will look at the writings of the early church leaders to find how

God spoke to us through them about cross-cultural communication.

Christ's Incarnation

In John 1: 1-14, the incarnation of Jesus Christ is described. This act supports cross-cultural ministry. Verse 14 states that: "The Word became flesh and made his dwelling among us. We have seen his glory, the glory of the one and only, who came from the Father, full of grace and truth. " Special emphasis is given to "The Word became flesh and made his dwelling among us." Theologian David Fergusson states that: "Following the prologue of the Fourth Gospel, the Christology of the early church was shaped by the thought that the logos, the pre-existent Son of God, had become a human being in the person of Jesus of Nazareth" (Fergusson, 75). Philippians 2:6-8a affirms John's statement:

> Who, being in very nature of God, did not consider equality with God something to be grasped, but made himself nothing, taking the very nature as a servant, being made in human likeness. And being found in appearance as a man..."

The fact that God became man in Christ for the purpose of revealing Himself to human beings takes center stage in the Church's understanding of cross-cultural ministry and communication. The truth is that Jesus left His heavenly kingdom and came to dwell with us, so that we may know our Heavenly Father. Gerald L. Borchert comments on John 1:14:

> The text means that the eternal Logos became human – truly human. The usual theological terminology used to describe this idea is that of the "incarnation" – an English construct word from Latin that has come to mean "God incorporated in flesh." (Borchert 1996, 119)

Roger L. Fredrickson writes:

> The word that was, the word that was with God, and the Word that was God – that word has become flesh. The living God has made His great decisive move in coming among us in the flesh! ... In this act of incarnation, eternity and time, the divine and the human, salvation and creation, are reconciled. By this act, He became subject to all the conditions of human existence – weakness, dependence, and morality which is our common lot. (Fredrickson, 43)

Merrill C. Tenney states:

> Christ entered into a new dimension of existence through the gateway of human birth and took up residence among men.... He left his usual place and accepted the conditions of human life and environment, with the

attendant temporal limitations that all humans experience. (Tenney, 33)

Mathew Henry comments:

> This intimates not only that he was really and truly man, but also that he subjected himself to the miseries and calamities of the human nature. He was made flesh, the meanest part of man… Wonder at this, that the eternal Word should be made flesh, when flesh was come into such an ill; that he who made all things should himself be made flesh, one of the meanest things, and submit to that from which he was at the greatest distance. (Henry, 143)

William Barclay writes:

> Perhaps as no where else in the New Testament, we have the full manhood of Jesus gloriously proclaimed. In Jesus we see the creating Word of God, the controlling reason of God, taking manhood upon Himself. In Jesus we see God living life, as God would have lived it if God had been a man. (Barclay, *John*, 45)

Indeed, Christ was willing to cross from His own culture (the heavenly kingdom) and live in the midst of a new culture (sinful mankind) in order to bring God's salvation to that new culture (which means He would suffer and die for the sins of mankind in order to provide eternal life for all). The gap between the sinful Christ and sinful man is a chasm that we can never fully comprehend. But Jesus' willingness to do this is God stating in the strongest terms that we must be willing to reach out to those different from ourselves for the sake of the Gospel; that we must be willing to understand and communicate with other cultures in order to take the Gospel to those cultures. David J. Hesselgrave and Edward Rommen write in their book, *Contextualization: Meaning, Methods, and Models* that: "Authenticity should have to do with God's revelation first of all, with faithfulness to the authority and content of the will of God revealed in his creation, in man's conscience, and especially, in his Son and his Holy Spirit- inspired Word" (Hesselgrave and Rommen, 199). Brian Hebblethwaite affirms that: "Though there could in principle be many incarnations of God claimed by other religions, there is only one realistic historical claim to such an incarnation, and that is the claim made for Jesus" (Hebblethwaite, 323).

H.R. Niebuhr has categorized five views of the relationship between Christ and this new culture that is used by many theologians:

1. Christ against culture - i.e., Christ is the sole authority; the claims of culture are to be rejected.
2. The Christ of culture - i.e., the Christian system is not different from culture in kind

but only in quality; the best of culture should be selected to conform to Christ.

3. Christ above culture - i.e., the reception of grace perfects and completes culture, though there is not a "smooth curve or continuous line" between them.

4. Christ and culture in paradox - i.e., both are authorities to be obeyed and the believer, therefore, lives with this tension.

5. Christ as Transformer of culture - i.e., culture reflects the fallen state of humanity; in Christ, humanity is redeemed and culture can be renewed so as to glorify God and promote his purposes. (Niehbur, 116)

This book affirms with Niebuhr that it is Christ who transforms the culture.

The incarnation of Jesus Christ is indeed a true example for the churches in the United States to follow in regard to cross-cultural ministry. Christ's culture (His life and teachings) can be understood and implemented by all churches in America. In fact, Sherwood G. Lingenfelter and Marvin K. Mayers in their book, *Ministering Cross-Culturally*, write that a central thesis of the New Testament is that it "speaks to all people and all cultures and that Jesus is the only faithful example of divine love in interpersonal relationships and communication" (Lingenfelter and Mayers).

<u>We Are All Kingdom Citizens</u>

All born again believers are Kingdom citizens, and they are not tied down to one culture or nationality. Fanyana P. Mhlophe comments on God and culture:

> God being completely unbound by any culture, he chooses to operate within a culture and, at the same time, outside culture. The Apostle Paul saw the need for the Gospel to cross cultural barriers when he insisted that Gentiles did not have to become cultural Jews before they become Christians. (Mhlophe, 54)

No matter where one travels around the globe, Christian faith is similar in all cultures. "The gospel is good news to all societies, and God has always called and is still calling his people to bear his redemptive love to every place and people group on the earth (Canales and Dufault, 34)." Herschel H. Hobbs states, "It is clear, therefore, that God regards men not by outward differences of race, culture, or economy, but by the inward condition of the heart (Hobbs, 22)." God's Kingdom is beyond culture, but, at the same time, is revealed within cultures. God's Kingdom supersedes all culture, cuts across all boundaries, and it is not tied down by any particular culture. Therefore, pastors and church leaders need to exercise legitimate sensitivity to all cultures because God loves all the people of the world equally.

The New Testament makes clear that the Kingdom of God is open to all persons. Acts chapter two demonstrates that the Good News of the Kingdom reaches across linguistic, nationalistic, ethnic, racial, and cultural barriers. Acts 2: 5-11 records the day of Pentecost as follows:

> Now there were staying in Jerusalem God-fearing Jews from every nation under heaven. When they heard this sound, a crowd came together in bewilderment, because each one heard them speaking in his own language. Utterly amazed, they asked: "Are not all these men who are speaking Galileans? Then how is it that each of us hears them in his own native language? Parthians, Medes and Elamites; residents of Mesopotamia, Judea and Cappadocia, Pontus and Asia, Phrygia and Pamphylia, Egypt and the parts of Libya near Cyrene; visitors from Rome (Both Jews and converts to Judaism); Cretans and Arabs ...we hear them declaring the wonders of God in our own tongues!

In Revelation 5: 9, we find that Christ's blood "purchased men for God from every tribe and language and people and nation." Again in Revelation 7: 9a, John reveals: "After this I looked and there before me was a great multitude that no one could count, from every nation, tribe, people and language, standing before the throne and in front of the lamb." All these scriptures indicate that God's Kingdom is given to all mankind. Dallas Willard asserts that: "We need a key to the keys. The abundance of God is not passively received, and does not happen to us by chance. We must act in union with the flow of God's Kingdom life that comes through our relationship with Jesus" (Willard, 57). It is a high time for all Christians to prepare for the Kingdom in spite of our denominational affiliation or cultural differences. The good news is that we will all be together in heaven with our Heavenly Father. Every born again Christian's destiny is heaven. Therefore, the focus of every believer should be how to lead as many people to Jesus Christ as possible. Our life's journey will end very soon. An average human lifespan is in the 70's, and we are accountable to God for how we spend those years. Our chance to do the Kingdom's work on earth is very short based upon our average span of life. We need to keep our focus toward heaven and do the Kingdom's work every day, leaving aside our earthly passions and short-sighted lifestyle.

Jesus and the Samaritan Woman

Jesus demonstrated this openness of God's kingdom in both His declaration and by His demonstration. There is no better example of this than in His encounter with the Samaritan woman that is described in John 4:1-42. The account begins with John stating that Jesus and His disciples were traveling from Judea to Galilee. John makes the statement about this journey that "he (Jesus) had to go through Samaria. So he came to a town in Samaria called Sychar" (vv. 4-5).

Why does John begin the story this way? Why would he point out that Jesus *had* to go through Samaria? Was there physically no other way for Jesus to lead His disciples from where they were to their new destination? This is not the case at all. While this would have been the quickest route to travel, a good Jewish leader like Jesus would have gone out of His way not to pass through Samaria for fear of being defiled by contact with the people who lived there (Tenney, 54). He would have traveled the longer route down from Jerusalem to the Jordan Valley, then along the Jordan River, and would have entered Jerusalem via the crossing at Beth Shan. While this route would also have brought the possibility of defilement by contact with Gentiles, most Jews would have chosen defilement by Gentiles as the lesser of the two evils. This was because the Samaritans were regarded by the Jews as despised half-breeds. When the Assyrians had destroyed the Northern Kingdom in 722 BC, they had sent many of the leading Jewish people into exile in other conquered lands while repopulating the Northern Kingdom with persons from the other conquered countries. The Jews who remained in the Northern Kingdom's territory intermarried with the new inhabitants from other places, thus ending their pure Jewish lineage. When Jerusalem was being rebuilt, in order to reestablish a pure and loyal people of God, Ezra put into place a policy that excluded Samaritans and others of mixed backgrounds from being considered part of the Jewish state (Ezra 9-10).

The antagonism between the groups had grown ever since that time (Borchert, 199-200).

The antagonism had reached such a height that Jews looked on the Samaritans with total contempt. One rabbinical statement was that any Jew who eats bread given him by a Samaritan "is as he who eats swine flesh." This Jewish-Samaritan quarrel had smoldered ever more bitterly and resentfully for over 400 years (Barclay *John*, 142), and Jesus was leading His disciples right into the middle of it.

Not only was He leading them, but He was compelled to do so. Not because it was the expedient route, but because it was the will of His Father. The word used in verse 4 for "had to" go through Samaria is the Greek word, *edei*. This word is generally used of Jesus to mean it was the divine will for him to do something. The passage through Samaria was willed by God. This is confirmed later in the story when Jesus tells His disciples in verse 34 that: "My food is to do the will of him who sent me and to finish his work" (Beasley-Murray, 59).

So why did Jesus have to pass through Samaria? Because God had a divine appointment He had to keep with a Samaritan woman. This appointment would have two results. One was the salvation of the woman and many other Samaritans in the city of Sychar (John 4:39-42). The other was to demonstrate to His disciples that He had come to bring good news to *all* people – even the hated Samaritans. Jesus would teach elsewhere the truth that the disciples had to reach out to persons of all cultures and backgrounds, including the despised Samaritans. One such place was the story of the Good Samaritan in Luke 10:30-37. In this parable, Jesus did the unthinkable and made a Samaritan the hero of the story (Tasker, 80). Teaching the truth is one thing; demonstrating it is another. Here, Jesus did the latter.

While Jesus ministered to the Samaritan woman, the disciples were off looking for food in the town (John 4:27, 31). Imagine their shock when they returned and saw Jesus talking to a Samaritan woman (John 4:27). She had three strikes against her in their time and culture: (1) she was a woman; (2) she was a Samaritan; (3) she was a woman with a questionable reputation (John 4:17-18). Yet Jesus was not bothered by any of this. He was reaching across all of these barriers to reach her and to teach these disciples that His message is for everyone, those of every culture and standing. As Gerald L. Borchert writes: "He was truly cross-cultural in his perspective and concern for others" (Borchert 1996, 210).

Jesus completes His teaching with two statements. Other Samaritans had heard the testimony of the woman Jesus had ministered to and were coming out of the city to meet with Him (John 14:28-30). As they came to where Jesus and the disciples conversed, all wearing their white robes, they may well have looked like a field of wheat ready for harvest (Barclay, 161). So Jesus may well have been observing this when He said, "Do you not say, 'Four months more and then the harvest?'"(John 4:35). This was probably a quotation of a proverb of the time (Tenney, 58). Then perhaps gesturing to the coming crowd all dressed in white, He added, "I tell you, open your eyes and look at the fields! They are ripe (or white, which is the literal translation) for harvest" (John 4:35). The crowd was the thus the harvest He was referring to (Barclay, 161). Jesus then tells His disciples that He had sent them "to reap what you have not worked for. Others have done the hard work, and you have reaped the benefits of their labor" (John 4:38). The disciples had been in town the entire time Jesus had been ministering to the woman. All these people coming to see Jesus had been in the town. The disciples would have had to have talked to many of them to find the food they had brought back and offered to Jesus (John 4:31). They had been ripe for harvest as the disciples had mingled among them. They had been prepared ahead of time by God. All they had to do was to tell them the Good News. Yet they had not done so. Had their prejudices against the Samaritans kept them from reaping what should have been an easy harvest? Had their unwillingness to reach across from their own culture to another caused them to miss an opportunity to serve God?

This must have had a great impact on the disciples. It should have a great impact on us also. We must not let our own misunderstandings, discomfort, and perhaps even prejudices keep us from ministering to every person in our community, regardless of their race, ethnicity, or socioeconomic background. Jesus taught His disciples that God's Kingdom is open to everyone, and as we will now see, these lessons continued to be taught in the life of the early Church after His ascension.

<u>Jesus Prays for Unity</u>

Jesus not only taught and practiced unity and cross-cultural ministry, He prayed for it. In John 17, Jesus prayed for His disciples and "for those also who believe in Me through their word" (v. 20). This means all of us who have accepted Jesus as our Savior and Lord. And what does Jesus pray for us? We find the answer in verses 21-23:

> "That all of them may be one, Father, just as you are in me and I am in you. May they also be in us so that the world may believe that you have sent me. I have given them the glory that you gave me, that they may be one as we are one: I in them and you in me. May they be brought to complete unity to let the world know that you sent me and have loved them even as you have loved me."

Jesus, the Son, and the Father model oneness. Therefore, when we become one with Christ, and through Christ with the Father, we also become one with each other. This is because we are then all indwelled with the same Father and Son through the Holy Spirit. This should lead to a unity among believers, but not a self-generated unity. This kind of unity cannot be manufactured by human efforts. It is the result of God at work. Therefore, when there is unity among believers, especially when it is among believers of greatly diverse cultures, it will allow the world to realize that God really does make a difference (Borchert 2002, 206-8). This then allows the church where there is real unity among a diverse group of people to have a powerful witness in its community.

Peter's Lesson Learned

As one of the key leaders of the early Church, it was vital that Peter learn and practice the truth of the cross-cultural nature of God's Kingdom. Acts 10:34-35 indicates that this indeed occurred: "Then Peter began to speak: 'I now realize how true it is that God does not show favoritism but accepts men from every nation who fear him and do what is right." Hobbs explains this verse as follows: "The phrase 'no respecter of person' may be rendered, 'God does not judge a man by his face.' Facial features reveal racial differences. And while man may look upon outward appearances, God looks upon the heart" (Hobbs, 22). I (Louis) was reminded of an incident during my college days. I was attending an International student organization meeting. In this meeting, they were electing officers for the organization, such as president, secretary, and treasurer. I was new to the organization and did not know all the students. A friend nominated me to be the secretary, but then a tall guy made a comment that I was too short. The people just laughed at that remark and the case was closed. In this situation, just because I was not tall like him, I could not be one of the officers for the organization. In general, the outward appearance does carry a lot of weight in the social sector, political arena, and even in religious circles. In this world, it is our human nature to look upon outward appearances, but how good it is to be able to rest assured that our Heavenly Father looks at our heart.

In The New American Commentary, John B. Polhill comments that Peter is emphasizing:

> That God shows no favoritism, accepts people from every nation, and that Jesus is "Lord of all." This emphasis on the universal gospel is particularly suited to a message to Gentiles. Peter's vision had led him to this basic insight that God does not discriminate between persons, that there are no divisions between "clean" and "unclean" people from the divine perspective. The Greek word used for favoritism is constructed on a Hebrew idiom meaning on the basis of race or ethnic background, looking up to some and down on others. (Polhill, 260)

Barnes in his commentary explains the same reference:

> The barrier is broken down; the offer is made to all; God will save all on the same principle; not by external privileges or rank, but according to their character. The sense is that he now perceived that the favors of God were not confined to the Jew, but might be extended to all others on the same principle. Acceptance with God does not depend on the

fact of being descended from Abraham, or of possessing external privileges, but on the state of the heart. (Barnes, *Acts*, 177)

John Stott writes that Peter's revelation is "that God's attitude to people is not determined by any external criteria, such as their appearance, race, nationality or class. There is no racial barrier to Christian salvation" (Stott 1990, 189-90). F. F. Bruce adds that in this declaration, Peter is:

Sweeping away the racial prejudices of centuries. It was plain, then, that God had no favourites as between one nation and another, but any man who feared Him and acted rightly was acceptable to Him, no matter what nation he belonged to. (Bruce, 224-5)

The Scriptures clearly explain that God's Kingdom is for all the people in the world. There is no sign of prejudice in God's Kingdom but equal citizenship. Therefore, even here on earth, the church's ministry needs to be sensitive to the clear message of crossing over from one's own culture and reaching out to other cultures to share the Good News.

This was a precept that Peter had to learn. This passage in Acts 10 comes at the end of a lesson God had to teach him so that he would be ready to minister to the Gentile Cornelius. The church's mission had steadily been broadening and it was time for the gospel to be presented across the barrier between Jews and Gentiles (Longenecker, 383). By the end of Acts 10, not only had Peter led Cornelius and his family to Christ, but he had become committed to the cross-cultural Gentile mission. His commitment would lead to the church's commitment to this mission. This is why Polhill cites Acts 10 as marking "a high point in the church's expanding mission" (Polhill, 249). It is why William Barclay calls it "one of the great turning points in the history of the church" (Barclay, *Acts*, 82).

Peter demonstrated that he had learned the importance of reaching across cultures to the Gentiles when he defended Paul and Barnabas' ministry to the Gentiles in Acts 15:7-11. He concluded his defense with these words: "He (God) made no distinction between us and them, for he purified their hearts by faith" (Acts 15:9). While Peter's story was another example of God's emphasis on the need to take the gospel across cultures, it also shows how difficult this ministry can be. For all of his growth in this area, Peter still struggled with it at times. He was pulled back into his previously prejudicial views when influenced by the peer pressure of fellow Jewish believers while he was in Antioch (Galatians 2:11-13). The result was that Paul had to "oppose him to his face" Galatians 2:11) to get him back on the right track.

Paul's Emphasis on Unity in the Body of Christ

Paul's ministry was cross-cultural. This self-proclaimed "Hebrew of Hebrews" (Philippians 3:5), also said, "I am the apostle to the Gentiles" (Romans

11:13). God Himself said about Paul: "This man is my chosen instrument to carry my name before the Gentiles" (Acts 9:15). God had chosen a committed Jew to reach across cultural barriers and to be the main tool for reaching the Gentiles. As part of his understanding of the cross-cultural nature of his ministry, Paul emphasized often the oneness and unity of all believers no matter what their heritage.

Paul consistently taught that among believers in Christ, unity in Christ supersedes the cultural barriers which divide people. Under his leadership, the New Testament church became multicultural in nature. The writers of *Multi-Ethnicity* explain:

> We must remember our identity as the body of Christ and recognize that we have missed out on God's blessing by keeping ourselves separate from one another. Jesus' desire is that his body function together, each member empowering the other in ministry. (Canale and Dufault, 41)

In referring to unity in Christ across culture and all other barriers, Hobbs declares: "Use any combination of races, nationalities, or culture and economic classes, and the answer is the same... two Christian brothers" (Hobbs, 40). The classic Pauline text referring to the unity of the Body of Christ is 1 Corinthians 12:12-17. Nevertheless, there are many other scriptures which are even more specific regarding unity in Christ irrespective of racial, linguistic, ethnic, or cultural barriers.

In dealing with enmity between Jew and Gentile in Ephesians 2:14-18, Paul writes:

> For he himself is our peace, who has made the two one and has destroyed the barrier, the dividing wall of hostility, by abolishing in his flesh the law with its commandments and regulations. His purpose was to create in himself one new man out of the two, thus making peace, and in this one body to reconcile both of them to God through the cross, by which he put to death their hostility. He came and preached peace to you who were far away and peace to those who were near. For through him we both have access to the Father by one Spirit.

Paul continues to explain in Ephesians 3:6 that "through the gospel the Gentiles are heirs together with Israel, members together of one body, and sharers together in the promise in Christ Jesus." Again in Ephesians 4: 4-6, it is clearly stated that:

> There is one body and one Spirit ... Just as you were called to one hope when you were called ... one Lord, one faith, one baptism. One God and Father of all, who is over all and through all and in all.

This means the community, the Messiah, and the one God are mutually explanatory realities.

Other primary Pauline texts that support the unity of the Body of Christ across culture and all other barriers are Galatians 3:26-29:

> You are all sons of God through faith in Christ Jesus, for all of you who were baptized into Christ have clothed yourselves with Christ. There is neither Jew nor Greek, slave nor free, male nor female, for you are all one in Christ Jesus. If you belong to Christ, then you are Abraham's seed, and heirs according to the promise.

And Colossians 3:11: "Here there is no Greek or Jew, circumcised or uncircumcised, barbarian, Scythian, slave or free, but Christ is all, and is in all." Most commentators are in agreement about the emphasis in Galatians 3:26-29, with special reference to verse twenty-eight. Timothy George remarks, for example: "The redemptive work of Christ and incorporation into his body have relativized the former distinctions of race, rank, and role" (George, 274). James Montgomery Boice states that "having become one with God as his sons, Christians now belong to each other in such a way that distinctions that formerly divided them lose significance" (Boice, 468). Skip Ryan affirms this by writing: "The church is called the people of God or the body of Christ" (Ryan, 61).

R. A. Cole, in the Tyndale series of commentaries, states:

In the collective whole which is 'the body of Christ' there is no longer any place for the traditional distinctions that divide mankind … culture, linguistic, religious or sexual. Paul bases his strong position (the abolition of such distinctions) on the grounds that all are now his, 'one man' or 'an entity', in Christ. Here again is the concept of the collective whole. It is a short step from this to the use of the 'body- concept', which sees the totality of believers as the body of Christ. (Cole, 110-11)

Richard N. Longenecker explains the passage, writing:

So it may be surmised that in conscious contrast to such Jewish and Greek chauvinistic statements, early Christians saw it as particularly appropriate to give praise in their baptismal confession that through Christ the old racial schisms and cultural divisions had been healed. (Longenecker, 157)

Longenecker adds that when early Christians wrote that when the early believers spoke of being into Christ:

They also spoke of the old divisions between Jew and Gentile, slave and free, and male and female having come to an end... these three couplets also cover in embryonic fashion all the essential relationships of humanity, and so need to be seen as having racial, cultural, and sexual implications as well. (Longenecker, 157)

Longenecker concludes: "Paul finds the essence of the Christian proclamation: that 'in Christ Jesus' there is a new 'oneness' that breaks down all former divisions and heals injustices" (Longenecker, 158).

Colossians 3:11 could be described using the words of Peter T. O'Brien, who states: "Within this new humanity the barriers that divided people from one another, racial, religious, cultural and social are abolished" (O'Brien, 192). Robert W. Wall explains more fully that this is a Pauline "Magna Carta" of the sort we find in Galatians 3:28. The sociology of the faith community found in Christ is egalitarian. God does not play favorites; God saves us all in the same way and for the same end. Thus, the divisions Paul draws here represent religious (Jewish) and cultural (Hellenistic) classes (Wall, 144). Jesus, a true Israelite, came for the sake of the Kingdom of God. That is what his preaching, his life and ministry, and his death and resurrection were all about (Rottenberg, 7-13).

E. K. Simpson and F. F. Bruce give a precise commentary on Colossians 3:11:

It is not only the old habits and attitudes that are abolished in this new creation. The barriers that divided men from one another are abolished as well. There were racial barriers, like that between Gentiles and Jew (that was a religious barrier too, as the reference to circumcision and uncircumcision indicates). There were cultural barriers, which divided Scythians and other barbarians from those who shared in the Graeco-Roman civilization of the Mediterranean world. There were social barriers, such as that between slaves and freedom. Outside the Christian fellowship these barriers stood as high as ever and there were Christians on the one side and on the other. From the viewpoint of the old order these Christians were new creation - "in Christ"- these barriers were irrelevant; indeed, they did not exist....This restoration of the original image of creation will be universally displayed on the day when the sons of God are revealed; but how good and pleasant it is when, as far as in us lies, we can display it in our Christian brotherhood here and now as an example to this divided world far more eloquent than all our preaching, so that men are constrained to confess, as they did in earlier days: "See how these Christians love one another!" (Simpson and Bruce, 274-78)

Paul also relates this focus on the unity of all believers in spite of their backgrounds in terms of God as One who does not play favorites. He writes, for example, to the church in Rome that "God does not show favoritism" (Romans 2:11), and to the church at Ephesus "that there is no favoritism with him (God)" (Ephesians 6:9). James concurs with Paul and takes the next logical step of stating that if we show favoritism, therefore, it is sin (James 2:9).

Paul demonstrated his application of the need for unity among all Christians and the need to reach out to all unbelievers, even if it means reaching across cultures in 1 Corinthians 9:19-23. In this passage, he states that he makes himself "a slave to everyone to win as many as possible" (v. 19). He states his cross-cultural method by writing that "to those under the law I became like one under the law (though I myself am not under the law), so as to win those under the law" (v. 20). He concludes with the familiar passage: "I have become all things to all men so that by all possible means I might win some" (v. 22). These verses show clearly that Paul not only believed cross-cultural ministry was part of God's plan, but that he practiced cross-cultural ministry as well. As William Barclay writes about Paul in this passage:

> This is not a case of being hypocritically two-faced and of being one thing to one man and another to another. It is a case, in the modern phrase, of being able to get alongside anyone. The man who can never see anything but his own point of view, who is completely intolerant, who totally lacks the gift of sympathy, who never makes any attempt to understand the mind and heart of others, will never make a pastor or an evangelist or even a friend... so long as we make no effort to understand

> (people), so long as we make no attempt to find some point of contact, we can never get anywhere with them. Paul, the master missionary, who won more men for Christ than any other man, saw how utterly essential it was to become all things to all men. One of our greatest necessities is simply to learn the art of getting alongside people; and the trouble so often is that we do not even try (Barclay, *Corinthians*, 93-4).

These passages confirm Paul's emphasis on the importance of the unity of the church so that God's good news can be spread to all cultures. This emphasis on unity for evangelism's sake leads to another reason that cross-cultural ministry is so crucial to God's purposes. There can be no Great Commission without cross-cultural ministry.

The Missiological Understanding of the Gospel

To fulfill the missiological understanding of the Gospel, one must understand God's heart for multicultural ministry. We see this from His call of Abraham to be the father of His called aside nation. Abraham was an immigrant. He experienced the stresses associated with adapting to a new and different culture. As Dixie L. Hunke writes:

> Abraham faced the same challenges that newcomers encounter today. According to Hebrews 11:9-10, he was a foreigner, living

in a tent which was pitched outside the city gates. His situation was transitory. He was vulnerable to dangers and experienced discrimination. But he looked forward to a better day. (Hunke, 3)

Not only did God call an alien to birth His people, but in the midst of that call, He made it clear that He was setting aside this people to do cross-cultural ministry. God said to Abraham:

I will make you into a great nation and I will bless you; I will make your name great, and you will be a blessing. I will bless those who bless you, and whoever curses you I will curse; and all peoples on earth will be blessed through you. (Genesis 12:2-3)

Kenneth A. Mathews writes about this passage:

The promissory call is the first recorded speech since God's word of judgment at the Tower of Babel, resulting in the creation of the nations.... This new word to Abram counters the old since it provides for the redemptive plan of "all peoples" (v. 3). By making his descendents a "great nation" (v. 2) who will be a "blessing" (v. 2), the Lord will bring salvation to the scattered nations. (Matthews, 105)

This emphasis on ministry across cultures can also be observed when God gives His law for His people through Moses. In Deuteronomy 10: 19, for example, God states: "And you are to love those who are aliens, for you yourselves were aliens in Egypt." In a *Christianity Today* article entitled "Here Comes the World," Tim Stafford has this to say regarding immigration:

> Ethnic diversity appears, by the light of the Book of Revelation, to be eternal. At the final consummation of history, it is announced that God will live with men, and "they will be his people" (Revelation 21:3). (The Greek is plural). Later it is said that the nation will walk by the light of the Lamb (21:24). People from all nations, however, will be united in worship before the throne of God, a great multitude "from every nation, tribe, people and language' (7:9). This will be the great and final immigration. (Stafford, 25)

To minister effectively Christian leaders need to be very much aware of the needs of all cultures. The best way to reach others whose culture is different with the gospel of Christ is through ministry that is sensitive to their unique background and that is multicultural in nature. Michael G. Maudlin comments that: "The church has got to understand that if we're going to be relevant in the modern age, you've got to be creative in presenting the message" (Maudlin, 44).

The Old Testament prophets also spoke of the need for multicultural ministry. Isaiah clearly testifies:

Let no foreigner who has bound himself to the Lord say, "The Lord will surely exclude me from his people." And let not any eunuch complain, "I am only a dry tree." For this is what the Lord says: "To the eunuchs who keep my Sabbaths, who choose what pleases me and hold fast to the covenant – to them I will give within my temple and its walls a memorial and a name better than sons and daughters; I will give them an everlasting name that will not be cut off. And foreigners who bind themselves to the Lord to serve him, to love the name of the Lord, and to worship him, all who keep the Sabbath without desecrating it and who hold fast to my covenant—these I will bring to my holy mountain and give them joy in my house of prayer. Their burnt offerings and sacrifices will be accepted on my alter; for my house will be called a house of prayer for all nations. (Isaiah 56:3-7)

C. F. Keil and F. Delitzsch comment:

Throughout this passage the spirit of the law is striving to liberate itself from its bondage. Nor is there anything to surprise us in the breaking down of the party wall, built up so absolutely between the eunuchs on the one hand and the congregation on the other, or the one partially erected between the heathen and the congregation of Israel; as we may see from Ch. Lxvi. 21, where it is affirmed that

Jehovah will even take priests and Levites out of the midst of the heathen whom Israel will bring back with it into its own land. (Keil and Delitzsch, 363)

Keil and Delitzsch continue to explain: "Not only is there no ground for supposing that Gentiles who love Jehovah will be excluded from the congregation; but it is really Jehovah's intention to gather some out of the heathen, and add them to the assembled diaspora of Israel" (Keil and Delitzsch, 364).

Geoffrey W. Grogan remarks: "In this way there is a practical translation of the missionary vision of chapters 40-55 into modest terms, in the midst of Israel" (Grogan, 315). He continues to relate: "The very one whose purpose involves gathering his own scattered people will include the foreigners too in the great pilgrimage to Jerusalem" (Grogan, 316).

Barnes notes about this passage that it states the following idea about persons of various backgrounds: "they should be admitted to the same privileges with those who had been long recognized as the people of God.... It is designed to intimate that hereafter all such barriers be broken down.... There is to be no assumption of superiority of one nation or rank over another" (Barnes, *Isaiah*, 307).

As we move to the New Testament, the best text to support the biblical call to multicultural ministry as part of the mission work God gives to His people is Matthew 28: 19-20:

Therefore go and make disciples of all nations, baptizing them in the name of the Father and of the son and of the Holy Spirit, and teaching them to obey everything I have commanded you. And surely I am with you always, to the very end of the age.

Commenting on the thrust of the passage, Barnes notes:

This gracious commission was the foundation of their authority to go to the Gentiles. The Jews had expected that the offers of life under the Messiah would be confined to their own nation. Jesus broke down the partition wall, and commissioned his disciples to go everywhere, and bring the world to the knowledge of himself. (Barnes, *Matthew*, 177)

Sherman E. Johnson comments as follows on the Great Commission:

We need not long pause to ask how the sense of world mission came to the early church. It may have been mediated through the failure of the plea of Jewry, but it came from the lips and life of Christ. All nations are a recurrent theme in his teaching. Let the reader trace the word "world" through his recorded words. In an age of narrow loyalties, when national prejudices were sharpened into animosity and often into contempt, Jesus ranged the world both in the gifts of his love and the yearning of his gospel. "One world" made its bid for a time to become an accepted slogan, the expression of a recognized necessity; but, had we listened, we could have heard it long ago from Christ. (Johnson and others, 622)

D. A. Carson explains:

A good case can be made for saying that the full expression *panta ta ethne*, used four times in Mathew (24:9, 14; 25: 32; here), uses *ethne* in its basic sense of "tribes," "nations," or "peoples" and means "all peoples" [without distinction] or "all nations' [without distinction]." Matthew's Gospel is now, in its final verses, returning to the theme introduced in the very first verse (see on 1:1) – that the blessings promised to Abraham and through him to all peoples on earth (Genesis 12: 3) are now to be fulfilled in Jesus the Messiah. And when that covenant promise is reiterated in Genesis 18:18; 22:18, the LXX uses the same words found here: *panta ta ethne*. (Carson, 596).

There can be no compromise under any conditions in the fulfilling of God's purpose to share the Good News to all nations. Therefore, it is the responsibility of all clergy and laymen to spread the Good News around the world. Joan Delaney states that: "A pilgrimage in mission involves the rejection of the possibility of a lucrative career as well as a certain denial of physical comfort, all for the specific purpose of the conversion both of oneself and of others" (Delaney, 26). Peter C. Phan comments in regard to Western Christian ministry:

> It is true that it has long lost hegemony, but numerically Christians, who still exercise a powerful influence on Western society, constitute by far the majority of believers. It goes without saying that all these commonalities – linguistic, cultural, politico-economic, and religious – simplify somewhat the task of adapting the Christian faith to the contemporary society in the West. (Phan, 724-5)

On the other hand, Laurenti Magesa states that contemporary men and women are living in a time when, surely as never before in the history of human existence, the world has been brought together by science and technology into something like a single household (Weber, 201).

Conclusion

Christ's incarnation to this world enables us to understand the love of God and His desire to see the redemption of all mankind. This includes people of all cultures and nationalities. The thrust of cross-cultural ministry in the United States, or wherever it may be in the world, is to fulfill the Kingdom's vision. The finality of the believer's eternal home is to be in God's Kingdom, as Kingdom citizens. No ministry in the world can be effective without unity in the Spirit as Christ's church. Unity in the Body of Christ enables believers to cross the boundaries of one's cultural barriers, and unites believers to work together for the Kingdom's sake. Faithfulness to God's Word, including reaching out to all lost persons, is the reason a believer needs to be cross-cultural and to seek unity among all believers of all cultures. As Milton Massie and Marc Hinkel state it:

> I believe there are few other issues to consider when deciding upon an effective motivation for involving oneself in the process of biblical unity. ..That is, true and biblical unity in the body of Christ across racial barriers could result in one of the most effective witnesses to win the lost for Christ that the world has ever seen. (Massie and Hinkel, 95-96)

The overall theological foundation that has been discussed in this chapter will not have an impact unless it is understood ultimately as a missiological mandate to all born again believers. The impact it should have is to mobilize the church into action. Theology that does not lead to action is meaning-less. The action that should be the result of a biblical theology is to reach out with the Gospel message to all the persons in a church's community, no matter what their culture. A multicultural church will reach people that no other type of church can reach. It will reach people such as interracially married families, international students and business people and their families, people who are used to working and living in a culturally diverse setting, "third culture kids" (children such as missionary or military children who have grown up among another culture or many other cultures and so do not consider any one culture their own), people having a hard time finding others like themselves, and people who are just tired of all the separation and ethnocentricity they see in our society, including many churches (Goette). Thus it is imperative that we have multi-cultural churches. The rest of this book will provide ideas for putting this theology to work in the church by reaching across cultural barriers so that churches can faithfully follow the teachings of our Lord.

CHAPTER 2

FOUNDATIONAL TRUTHS FOR MULTICULTURAL MINISTRY

Introduction

B efore we look at some tools for practicing cross-cultural ministry, we must first come to understand some foundational truths about this type of ministry. These truths are based on the biblical principles already discussed, as well as the observations of those involved in cross-cultural ministry regarding the practical realities of this type of ministry. Thus these concepts come from the hard work of studying Scripture and studying other cultures. If these ideas are not grasped, then it will be very difficult to successfully minister cross-culturally, and through that ministry develop a multicultural church.

Cross-Cultural Ministry Requires Being Biblical

The beginning place for all we do as Christians must be God's Word. We must be willing to learn about and from other cultures; we must be willing to make adaptations so that we can minister to and with persons of all cultures; we must never, however, do this at the cost of compromising biblical truth. We must never insist on our own personal preferences and values being followed, but we must insist on biblical truth being followed. As Karl Rennstich writes: "The only absolute values to which every culture must bow are the eternal biblical values to which Jesus held. These are the values above time and above culture, not bound by culture, but which should penetrate and re-form culture" (Rennstich). Cross-cultural ministry will require adaptation on our part. However, we must remember that adaptation cannot contradict Scripture. Scott Moreau reminds us that:

> On the one hand we must mold the faith in such a way that it is understood within the idioms of each culture. On the other hand we must guard against diluting or changing the faith in such a way that eternal truths are compromised or lost. (Moreau, 27)

The reason this is true is because of what Scripture teaches about itself. It teaches that Scripture is God's Word. It is written by men, but these men were inspired by God to make certain we received exactly the truth He wanted us to receive. The Holy Spirit worked in the hearts and minds of these men God chose so that He got written exactly what He wanted us to receive. This means that God's Word contains God's exact truth and is therefore authoritative in the life of all Christians (Psalm 19:7-8; John 17:17; 2 Timothy 3:16-17; 2 Peter 1:21).

If the Bible is indeed God's Word, is completely true and trustworthy, and is authoritative, then it is true for all believers, no matter what their cultural background (Romans 1:16; 10:12; 1 Corinthians 1:21-24; Galatians 3:27-29; Colossians 3:8-17). This means all Christians from all backgrounds are to believe and practice what it teaches. Thus Scripture becomes the yardstick by which we must measure any ministry we are involved in, including adapting to minister cross-culturally. We have no right to impose our views, values, or ways on anyone, but we do have a responsibility to hold everyone of every culture – beginning with ourselves and our own culture – to the truths of God's Word.

Scripture itself calls us to be cross-cultural. It calls us to be willing to adapt to minister to and with other cultures. It teaches that we can and must do things in different ways to relate to others for the sake of God's kingdom. Therefore, we are being biblical when we minister cross-culturally and are willing to adapt to do so. We have already seen this in the previous chapter when we discussed Peter and a willingness to eat food forbidden in the Old Testament law (Acts 10). As we also saw in Chapter 1, Paul wrote of the need to adapt to minister to other cultures without compromising the truth of Scripture in 1 Corinthians 9:19-23.

We must be biblical if we are going to minister cross-cultural. First, this will motivate us to be cross-cultural. The Bible will give us the call and the motivation to be cross-cultural. It will lead us to accurately discern the views of other cultures so we can better build bridges to its members. It will at the same time make certain that we do not compromise God's absolute truths; that we do not affirm the legitimacy of any worldview that contradicts those truths in our zeal to reach out to others (Psalm 1:1; Galatians 1:9; Colossians 2:8).

Cross-Cultural Ministry Requires Commitment

Multicultural ministry goes against our grain as human beings. It is natural for most of us to want to stay within our own comfort zone. We all believe that our culture is the best. It is the culture in which we have been raised. Most of us have even been taught from birth that our culture's way is the best way. We call this ethnocentrism. Sociologist David Popenoe defines this as the "tendency to evaluate other cultures in terms of one's own and to automatically evaluate one's own culture as superior" (Popenoe, 65). Many sociologists believe that ethnocentrism can serve a positive function in societies because if people believe the values and norms of their culture are good and right, they are more likely to conform to them and thus be good citizens. This helps bring about social order and stability (Popenoe, 65-6).

While this may be true, ethnocentrism also makes it difficult for churches to reach out those of cultural backgrounds different than that of the majority in the church.

Therefore as believers, we must overcome this type of ethnocentrism. If we are convinced that multicultural ministry is an effective way to reach our ever more diverse American population, then we must be willing to step out of our comfort zone to reach out to people different from ourselves. "While being strong proponents of our tradition, we must be stronger proponents of doing what it takes to bring the good news message to those who have yet to believe" (Pocock and Henriques, 37). As Kingdom citizens living in a multicultural world, "the challenge is to accept differences in others and even to be multicultural, that is, to be able to walk from our own culture into the culture of others" (Lingenfelter and Mayers, 11).

We must also concede that this is not easy. It is a stretching experience for us. It stretches us emotionally, relationally, and spiritually. It causes us to have to live on the edge, risking ourselves in an unfamiliar context. Some have referred to this as culture shock. Culture shock is defined by Paul Hiebert as the "the sense of confusion and disorientation we face as we move into another culture" (Hiebert, 37). Marvin Mayers says it is "that emotional disturbance which results from adjustments to a new cultural environment" (Meyers, 192). This culture shock can cause a conflict between the norms of the person reaching out to a new culture with the norms of that new culture.

The result is a feeling of tension that causes us to have to live on the edge of our comfort zone.

Living on the edge is not a comfortable place for most of us. When it comes to cross-cultural living on the edge, most of us have a fear of heights. I (David) remember the first time I went to New York City and visited the Empire State Building. As I stood on the observation deck at the top of the building, I looked over the edge and suddenly had an overwhelming sense of fear. I ran for the wall far away from the edge and stood there with my back firmly planted against that wall until my wife enticed me to face my fear and come closer to the edge so I could enjoy the view. I had the same overwhelming sense of fear the first time I visited a foreign country that was not English speaking. I stood in a Honduran airport by myself. Everyone around me was speaking Spanish. I suddenly began wondering what would happen if I could not find someone to translate for me and help me through the process of getting through customs. I began to feel panic and wondered why I had agreed to come and work with the missionaries there. I was never so glad in my life to hear a man call my name and speak English to me. It was one of the missionaries who had come to meet me. I was on the cross-cultural edge and it was not comfortable. In fact, it was at times terrifying. But by the time the trip was over, I knew I had made the right choice by turning my fear over to the Lord, stepping out of my comfort zone, and being willing to minister in a culture different than my own. We must make the same determination here in our own neighborhoods in the United States.

Cross-cultural ministry is also uncomfortable because it means that we will not be able to do church exactly the way we are used to or would like to. Tom Maluga states that "the variety of cultures in a church enriches the membership even though achieving unity may mean no one gets to experience church exactly the way they like it" (Lawson, 19). I (David) know that when our multicultural church first began to use songs in other languages and styles or when our pastor would stop and explain a point in another language, I would feel uncomfortable. But as time went on, it became part of the way I worshipped and today it seems strange to sit in a more traditional completely English language service. The key was that I had made a commitment to our church's multicultural vision and I was willing to step out in faith and trust God that He would help me overcome my misgivings.

This type of discomfort is not easily overcome. This is why we as leaders must recognize that the people we lead will need help in this. We must be patient and loving with them. It must also be recognized that overcoming fear and discomfort to reach across cultures is true not only for we in the church as we attempt to reach out, but also to those we are attempting to reach out to. We must challenge the people we lead with God's Word. Our most fervent pleas and inspiring rhetoric will not persuade people to be willing to step beyond their comfort zones and reach out to people of other cultures. This is a heart issue that only God's Word can touch and change.

We who are leaders must not only ask for commitment from those we serve, but we must also lead by example. We must be willing to do the hard things and make the hard changes necessary to help reach other cultures. One aspect of this is our commitment to remain through the process; to stick it out at the church even when things get rough. Too many ministers begin changes in churches and then when things become difficult they move elsewhere. Ministers who want to bring any change in a church, especially one of the magnitude necessary to reach out to other cultures, must be willing to make the commitment to God and His church to see the process through to its end, realizing that it probably will be a long, difficult endeavor.

Cross-Cultural Ministry Requires Patience

When God gives us a clear picture from His Word of what direction our church should take, we want the people in the church to immediately be on board and follow this leadership. We must remember, however, that change never comes easily. This is especially true when it comes to reaching out to other cultures. Leading people through change always takes love and patience. Remember from the last chapter that even Peter took time to get the message of God's desire to reach out to the Gentiles. Even when he "got it," he still reverted to his old ways at times and had to be reminded forcefully by Paul of God's desire. Therefore, we must begin the process of leading our churches to reach out to other cultures with that commitment we just talked about to patiently work through the process no matter how long it takes. When we are confident something is God's will, we are able to do this.

Church planter Robert Goette presents five stages that most organizations, including churches, must go through in order to change to be able to effectively reach out to persons from other cultures:

1. Many churches start with a *parochial view* that says, "Our way is the only way." They are open to persons from other cultures coming to their church as long as the persons from the other culture are willing to accept everything exactly as it already is. There is no willingness to change in order to reach out to persons from other cultures. It is expected that persons from other cultures should change if they want to be part of the church.

2. Churches usually move next to an "Our way is the best way" point of view, known as the *ethnocentric view*. Some churches may start here, but it is almost as difficult to reach other cultures from this view as it is from the first viewpoint. This view says there may not be anything particularly wrong with the other culture's ways of doing things, but our way is best, so it is best if we stay the way we are and they change to be more like us. Once again, the result is still very similar to the first view – others are welcome as long as they are willing to do things our way.

3. Churches may move to or start with the third stage, which states that "Our way is best for us; their way is best for them." This is a *polycentric view*. This viewpoint once again does not leave a church open to change. What usually occurs in such a church is that a separate church is started for persons from the other culture. They are welcome to join the "mother" church if they want, but they will have to do things "our" way. Otherwise, they are welcome to join the "mission" church where they are free to do things "their" way.

4. Churches next move to a *synergistic viewpoint*. This view states: "Our way and their way differ, and we can learn from each other." This way of thinking allows a church to be open to change, and is a sign that the church may truly be ready to begin reaching out to persons of other cultures. When people become willing to learn about other cultures, they are much more likely to be willing to make changes to make their church more appealing to persons from other cultures.

5. The final step is *multiculturalism*, where the church comes to believe that there is more than one way of doing things and we can not only learn from each other, but we do ministry and worship in many different ways as we learn from each other. When a church reaches this stage, they are open to making the necessary changes to reach and grow as Christians alongside people from other

cultures. Of course, Scripture is always the guide by which ideas from any culture are evaluated, but within those Scriptural boundaries, the church is open to making changes in worship style, methodology, etc. (Goette)

While churches must change, they are organizations composed of individual people. People also must go through a process of change so that they are open to reaching beyond their own comfort zone to minister to persons different from themselves. The reason it requires time and patience to lead a church through the process of change is because the people must go through a process themselves. Goette also presents stages that individuals must go through in developing cultural sensitivity. He offers two stages, each with three sub-stages as follows:

1. The *Ethnocentric Stage* is where most people begin. It is where they believe that their culture is absolutely right and therefore they are closed to the idea of change or even of trying to understand another culture. The idea of doing so has probably not even crossed their mind. Goette gives three sub-stages for this stage as follows:
    a. The sub-stage of *Denial* is where there is no recognition of cultural or other differences. The people in a church do not even think about other cultures. They are comfortable with their own culture and doing things their own way. There

not only is not a desire to reach out to people of other cultures, there is not even recognition of a need to do so. After all, if people of other cultures want to come to the church, they are welcome to do so. There is not even a thought that they may not feel comfortable or welcome if they did come.

b. The sub-stage of *Defense* is when people in the church begin to recognize minor differences between themselves and persons from other backgrounds in their community, but those differences are evaluated negatively. At this sub-stage there is at least a move toward recognizing the presence of persons different from themselves in the sphere of the church's influence, but there is not yet a willingness to admit that there is a need for the church to do anything different to reach out to those persons. The culture of the persons in the church is still viewed as "right" and, therefore, no effort is seen as needed to respond to differences with other cultures. Where there are differences, the other culture is seen as the one that needs to make changes to fit in with what the church is already doing. The members of the church feel a need to "defend" their way of doing things against the attacks of changes that might be necessary if the church was going to reach out to persons of other cultures.

c. The sub-stage of *Minimization* occurs when there is more recognition of differences between the culture represented in the church and other cultures in the community, and there is also an acceptance of at least superficial or minor differences. Examples of these minor differences are the types of food they eat or the style of clothes that they wear. They would be more outward, obvious differences. These would be differences that would not really require any change in the church members themselves, or in the way the church conducts its business. After all, persons from other cultures would be welcome even if they wanted to wear a different style of clothing or eat different food – they could even bring their type of food to a church meal.

2. The *Ethnorelative Stage* is where people in the church begin to move beyond just the recognition that there are other cultures in their community and that those cultures are different from that of the people in the church. They also begin to recognize that those differences are keeping the church from being effective at reaching a large portion of the people in their community. They recognize that those differences are holding the church back from fulfilling the Great

Commission given to it by Christ. There begins to be openness to making changes that are necessary so that the church can be an effective instrument in God's hands to reach all persons for Christ no matter what their background. According to Goette, there are three sub-stages in this stage:

a. The sub-stage of *Acceptance* brings more recognition and even some appreciation for differences in behavior and values of other cultures. It moves beyond just the superficial outward differences to an understanding of deeper differences such as relationship, conflict, learning, and leadership styles. There is recognition that these differences are not necessarily "bad" or "unwanted." They are not unbiblical, simply different than what the people in the church are used to. Therefore, they can be appreciated for their own value. This step allows there to at least be openness to the fact that some of these differences could be incorporated into the life of the church without damage to the church's integrity.

b. When the sub-stage of *Adaptation* is reached, there begins to be an understanding that because there are differences between the culture represented in the church and some cultures in the community the church is trying to reach, that changes need to take place if the church is going to have any influence in its community. This leads to the willingness by church members to develop the communication skills necessary to understand people of other cultures in the community better. Church members realize that they must communicate with persons from the differing cultures, so that they can understand them better, so that they can make changes in themselves and the church in order to more effectively minister to them.

c. The sub-stage of *Integration* brings the internalization by church members of the things they are learning about the other cultures. This means the members are beginning to incorporate some new ideas and methodologies into their own lives and into the life of the church. Once again, there is no compromise with biblical truth, but where changes make it easier to communicate God's truth, including the gospel message, they are put into practice, even if it means making changes in self or the church. The most important thing for church members becomes effectively ministering to all persons in the church's community, not feeling comfortable as individuals. (Goette)

One can see from reading about these stages – whether they are for individuals or entire churches

– that moving a church through them will take some time. Depending on where a church is at, we may have to teach church members what God teaches through His Word about reaching people from other cultures and about the equality of all persons. Then the church will have to learn about other cultures represented in its community and build relationships with people from those cultures. We will have to determine what changes we need to make and then make them. None of this will come easily or quickly. We must be patient and committed to the task. We must remember that God is patient with us and that He calls us to likewise be patient with each other. As He teaches us in His Word:

> Be devoted to one another in brotherly love. Honor one another above yourselves. Never be lacking in zeal, but keep your spiritual fervor, serving the Lord. Be joyful in hope, patient in affliction, faithful in prayer. (Romans 12:10-12)

> Be completely humble and gentle; be patient, bearing with one another in love. (Ephesians 4:2)

> Be patient with everyone. (1 Thessalonians 5:14)

> Be patient, then, brothers, until the Lord's coming. See how the farmer waits for the land to yield its valuable crop and how patient he

is for the autumn and spring rains. You too, be patient and stand firm, because the Lord's coming is near. Don't grumble against each other, brothers, or you will be judged. The Judge is standing at the door! Brothers, as an example of patience in the face of suffering, take the prophets who spoke in the name of the Lord. As you know, we consider blessed those who have persevered. You have heard of Job's perseverance and have seen what the Lord finally brought about. The Lord is full of compassion and mercy. (James 5:7-11)

This last passage from James is especially meaningful to cross-cultural ministry. While the specific reference is to patiently waiting through suffering to receive the rewards at Christ's return, it can also apply to faithfully serving God until we see His will take place, no matter how difficult it may be. James uses the farmer as an example of one who works patiently. The farmer must prepare the ground, sow the seed, tend the soil and plants, never really knowing what the weather may bring or what the crops may yield. The farmer patiently works and waits for what he considers a precious fruit. Is not what we labor and wait for – the conversion of all persons of all backgrounds to faith in Jesus Christ – much more precious (Richardson, 219)?

This passage not only calls us to be patient, but to "stand firm." It means literally to be steadfast in heart or mind (Zodhiates, 1313). This points to the truth that we must be strong in the inner man. We must come to the decision that what we are doing is based on God's Word and is, therefore, God's will. This will allow us to remain faithful no matter how difficult things become. Our confidence that we are acting in accordance with God's truth will undergird us when we feel weak, and will help us to persevere to the end (Burdick, 202). It is precisely what God was encouraging us with when he wrote in Galatians 6:9: "Let us not become weary in doing good, for at the proper time we will reap a harvest if we do not give up."

We must not only be patient with those in our church, but with those in the community that we are seeking to reach. Just as it is difficult for we in the church to be willing to leave our comfort zones and reach across to a different culture, it is also difficult for those we are seeking to reach out to. It may be even more difficult for them, because we have the help and prodding of the Holy Spirit working in our lives. If we are reaching out to unbelievers, they do not have that resource.

We must also remember that while we who are Americans may believe our culture and its ways are best, that persons from other countries do not necessarily feel that our way. They believe likewise that their culture is best. They may in fact have negative ideas about America and its culture. While they may hold the United States' technology, business skills, and material goods in awe, they are put off by the behavior of many Americans. They see them as having a superiority complex, as lacking values, and as being a culture that turns its back on history, traditions, and customs. Thus they have a very negative view of Americans and enter into any relationship with them with great hesitancy (North American Mission Board, 147; Stewart, 13-4).

Kalvero Oberg has identified five distinct stages through which persons from other cultures coming to America must pass through. These are as follows:

1. The *honeymoon phase* during which the person is excited about the new experience he is having. The sights, sounds, smells, and tastes all seem exhilarating. Any problems that are encountered are gladly accepted as part of the "experience."

2. The *rejection phase* comes fairly quickly – sometimes after only a few days – and lasts much longer than the honeymoon phase. Problems begin to seem much bigger. People in the new culture do not seem to understand why these problems are so big – after all, they are not a big deal to them. The newcomer begins to feel hostile toward and complains about the new culture and country. He notices only the bad and begins to feel extremely homesick.

3. The *regression phase* leads the newcomer to seek out others who are like himself. He looks for food from his home culture, videos from and about his home country. He only remembers the good about the old home. He wonders why he ever left. He wants nothing to do with the new country or its culture.

4. The *recovery phase* is where the newcomer begins to feel more at ease with the new culture. The customs do not seem as strange. The newcomer can move about the community fairly easily. He may still not understand all the nuances of the new culture's ways, but he understands enough to feel comfortable.

5. The *adjustment phase* is the final phase. Here the newcomer accepts completely the things of the new culture. He begins to appreciate their value. He accepts the customs, food, habits, etc. of the new culture. He understands that they are not better or worse than his own culture, simply different. (Addison)

As you can see, it can be just as difficult for persons from other cultures that live in our community. We must be patient with them as they adjust to their new experience. Depending on what phase they are in, it may take quite a while to be able to reach out to them. And if we do so while insisting that our way is the only way, we will not be successful.

This means that American church members must be willing to build relationships with people from other cultures. This takes great time and patience. But it is the only way for them to come to see that we are not the "ugly Americans" they may think we are. This will allow us to get below the surface differences so we can understand the deeper differences. This in turn will allow us to better minister to these persons from other cultures with greater effectiveness. It will allow us to truly demonstrate the love of Christ to them. This is a goal worth the time and effort it takes to accomplish.

Cross-Cultural Ministry Requires Prayer

Because reaching across cultures is such a challenge that requires such great commitment and patience, it also requires great amounts of prayer. William Willimon states that the spread of the gospel from the Jews to the Gentiles was nothing short of a miracle. He writes that "Luke knew that the thought of Gentile inclusion was so odd, so against the grain of Israel's conventional theological thinking, that nothing less than a miracle could explain so odd a lurch toward such offensive people as Cornelius, Agrippa, and the Ethiopian. Nothing less than the miracle of Acts 2 can explain such a move" (Willimon, 4). So while we will discuss in this book some specific strategies for reaching across cultures that can help us as we attempt to follow the biblical mandate to reach *all* people, we must realize that apart from the work of the Holy Spirit, those strategies will be fruitless. The Gentiles were only present in the early church at "the leading, prodding and gift of the Spirit" (Willimon, 4). The same is true of today's church moving out of its comfort zone to reach out to those different from ourselves.

If the Holy Spirit is the key to multicultural ministry, then prayer is the key biblically to accessing His power. Acts begins with Jesus' disciples waiting for the coming of the Holy Spirit as He directed them to after His resurrection (Luke 24:49; Acts 1:3-5). But they were doing more than just waiting. They were praying (Acts 1:12-14). It was as they prayed and waited on God that the Holy Spirit came and people of all nations were able to hear the gospel (Acts 2:1-12). As Willimon explains it:

> Waiting and praying signify the utter dependency of the disciples. The next move must be solely up to God, something like the resurrection itself. Empowerment will come as a gift, as a miracle, not through their efforts. Their challenge is not to become more conversant in the thought patterns of other cultures, but rather to be exclusively tethered to their Risen Lord. What they are asked to do is not a strategy for church growth, but rather the cultivation of a sense of dependency upon God to work for them what they cannot. (Willimon, 5)

Jesus had promised in Acts 1:8 that He would empower the disciples to evangelize and minister across cultures – their call was to go to all the nations. He fulfilled that at Pentecost, and that occurred after much prayer. This call continues to us today. We too need the power of the Spirit to minister to all people. Prayer is still the means to that power source. There are many excuses we can give for why we cannot reach out to other cultures – too many racial, ethnic, cultural, social, and economic barriers. It is true that these cannot be overcome through our own efforts. While better techniques for reaching out to others and greater sensitivity toward and understanding of other cultures may be helpful to us, they are not the only or most important element of cross-cultural ministry. As Willimon writes: "Cross-cultural hearing and comprehension is possible because God wills to make a way when, humanly speaking, there is no way" (Willimon, 6). That way is accessed through prayer.

I (Louis) experienced this power of prayer as I was working on this book. As I prayed over the book, I felt convicted to go to the United Nations compound and pray for all the nations. On October 18, 2005, I followed this conviction. As I stood at the United Nations, I was looking up to one flag at a time that flew there and praying for each nation represented by each flag. The flags start with Afghanistan and ends with Zimbabwe. Altogether, there are 191 countries flags hoisted in the United Nations compound. I was privileged to also take the tour inside the United Nations building. It was explained that the United Nation's goal is to have world peace. While the intentions of the United Nations are very impressive, I was convicted that only the Church of Jesus Christ has the means to bring this about. Only Christ can bring about the change in people's hearts that will allow them to live at peace with one another, just as the Jews and Gentiles were able to do in the New Testament.

I was convicted that it is high time for Christians in the United States to open their church doors to all the people of the world and welcome them to their churches. The Bible teaches about having love for one another. Jesus said: "'A new command I give you: Love one another. As I have loved you, so you must love one another. By this all men will know that you are my disciples, if you love one another.'" (John 13:34-35). The Bible also teaches about the source of real peace between persons. Paul writes: "For he himself (Jesus) is our peace, who has made the two one and has destroyed the barrier, the dividing wall of hostility" (Ephesians 2:14). The purpose of the church is not to be a social club, where a status is maintained and people of another culture or race are excluded. If we truly seek the Kingdom of God than it is clearly stated by Jesus Christ that it is prepared for all the people of the world that believe in Him. Jesus stated "that everyone who believes in him may have eternal life" (John 3:15).

It is the same challenge given to all the people of the world wherever you live. The Church's destiny is the Kingdom of God, which is open to all. Therefore all the believers of the world need to open their church doors to all the people in their community. One personal example is that of Agape College in Dimapur, India, where I (Louis) serve as the Founder and President. It is surrounded by many tribes of people who speak different dialects, and there are many non-Christians as well. We prayed for God's leadership in reaching out to our neighbors. The result has been that the college has recently started a Nagamese church on Sunday afternoons and they invite all the people in the community regardless of their ethnic or economic background. This is indeed true preparation for the Kingdom of God, and is preparation for ministry for those being trained at the college. These young men and women students who participate in this service will one day be leaders in churches. Prayerfully, this example will result in their leading the churches God makes them responsible for to reach out to people no matter what their background.

Cross-Cultural Ministry Requires Humility

The discussion often ensues in practicing cross-cultural ministry, or in the development of a multicultural congregation about which culture will dominate. But this should not be a concern at all. The question should not be which culture will dominate, but what is the best strategy to reach persons in a community while remaining true to biblical teaching. We must have the humility to be able to give up any conversation about one group of people dominating over another, especially any feeling that "our group" needs to be the one in control. This humility will demonstrate itself in several ways.

First, we must realize that we need to be willing to give up power to other persons, even persons of other cultural backgrounds. This may include submitting to the leadership of persons from another culture. Having persons in leadership positions in a church that represent the different cultures found in a community is important for several reasons. It shows that the church has accepted the biblical concept of multiculturalism; the idea that a church must reach out to and be open to all persons in a community.

It says to the community that this is a church that is truly open to all persons. It says that this church does not just give lip service to this idea, but that they are serious about it.

Scripture discusses the idea of power extensively (for example, in Matthew 20:20-28; Mark 10:35-45; Luke 22:24-27). There are many passages that speak to God's understanding of power and dominance. One of these passages is Luke 22:24-27. In this account of the final evening of Jesus with His disciples before His trial and crucifixion, the disciples begin to argue in the upper room immediately after the Lord's Supper about which of them was greatest. Jesus uses this as a teaching opportunity. He tells them that the Gentiles or sinners argue about such things. This is not to be an argument His disciples should ever have, because among His followers, greatness is not measured by being the one who is served, but by being the one who does the serving. Jesus says that He himself is their example for this, because "I am among you as one who serves" (v. 27). As Robert H. Stein writes:

> Greatness in the world's eyes involves being served by others. But Jesus had not come to be served but rather to serve. Although Jesus is clearly "greater" than the disciples, his behavior during his earthly ministry was one of serving them (cf. John 13:3-17; Phil. 2:6-11). Thus to be great in the kingdom means to follow Jesus and to become one who serves,

to think of oneself as having the least "rights."
(Stein, 548-9)

Another passage that clearly teaches Jesus' (and thus God's) attitude regarding greatness can be found in Luke 14:7-11. Here Jesus notices people at a banquet jockeying for the choice seats near the host. He warns his disciples that this should not be a practice of theirs. Instead they should purposely choose the seats of humility and lowliness. If the host then wants to call them to the seats of prominence, it is his choice to do so. Jesus concludes the teaching with these words: "For everyone who exalts himself will be humbled, and he who humbles himself will be exalted." Stein also comments on this passage saying that it teaches:

A general attitude toward self and others appropriate to members of God's kingdom (cf. 14:15). Meekness and humility are basic to the proper attitude believers should display in their relationship toward God ... Pride and arrogance are abominations before God. (This teaching) should be understood as a rejection of the proud, who exalt themselves, in favor of those who humble themselves. To know God is to understand both his infinite greatness and our own impotence and sinfulness. Pride is not possible under such circumstances. (Stein, 388, 390-1)

I (David) had to deal with this when our church decided to call a Hispanic pastor. Our community has a large Hispanic population and the Pastor Search Committee on which I served determined that we at least needed a pastor who spoke Spanish. When we offered this idea to the congregation, it was not met at first with enthusiasm. Some people were outwardly critical of the idea. The church leadership decided to spend some time teaching about the reasons for this – biblically and as a practical need in our community. We found a candidate who was of Hispanic background and who spoke both English and Spanish fluently. The church voted for him almost unanimously. While many people still were uncomfortable with the direction they saw the church going, they were willing to humble themselves, trust their concerns to God, and do what they had come to believe was pleasing to God. I must admit that I personally struggled with some of the changes that we made as this pastor came to lead our church. But I too had to swallow my pride and humble myself under his leadership because I believed he was the man God had put in that position, and I believed it was God's will that we reach all people in our community. Over time, God helped all of us overcome our concerns.

As this story indicates, humbling ourselves may well mean that we have to admit that we have been guilty of ethnocentrism – the idea that our culture and its ways are superior, and that persons of other cultures should do things our way. This is not easy to do. Just as it is not easy to submit to leadership that is different than we are used to, it is not easy to admit that we have been guilty of this type of prejudicial thinking. But as Jesus reminds us in Matthew 7:3-5, we have to be willing to look at ourselves first to see where we need to change before we can challenge others to change.

This also shows that we may have to admit that our way is not the best way at all. Others – even those from other cultures – may have ideas that are not only good, but that are better than our own. Acts 15:1-21 is an example of this from the life of the early church. Gentiles were being won to Christ through the ministry of Paul and Barnabas. The Jews thought that the only way to be a "good" Christian was to be circumcised and obey the Old Testament law. This caused a dispute to erupt between some of the key leaders of the early church based on cultural differences. Those of Jewish background thought their way – including circumcision as an essential element for following Christ – was best. Paul and Barnabas led a group who were convinced their way – including no need for circumcision – was best. The dispute led to a conference between the sides in Jerusalem, where a compromise solution was hammered out that allowed the ministry to the Gentiles to continue to prosper. Fortunately, both sides were willing to look to God to see what was essential, and they were willing to humble them-selves and submit to the teachings of God.

This humility was essential to the furtherance of the gospel among the Gentiles – a group quite cultur-ally different from the Jews in Jerusalem who were in the majority and who help the leadership positions in the church at the time of the events of Acts 15. As John B. Polhill points out:

> The ritual aspects of the law presented a problem....They were what made the Jews Jews and seemed strange and arbitrary to most Gentiles. To have required these of Gentiles would in essence have made them into Jews and cut them off from the rest of the Gentiles. It would have severely restricted, perhaps even killed, any effective Gentile mission. The stakes were high in the Jerusalem Conference. (Polhill, 324)

The stakes are equally high today. It would be just as devastating today for a church to be unwilling to humble itself and make adaptations to better reach out to persons of other cultural backgrounds in its community. The early church was open to the leadership of the Holy Spirit and this led to a humility that led to unity. This in turn opened the way for the mission of Paul to the Gentile world (Polhill, 321, 337). As Polhill states: "The Jewish Christian leadership showed a concern for the world mission of the church that overshadowed their own special interests. They took a step that was absolutely essential if the Gentile mission was to be a success" (Polhill, 337). The same must be said of us as we lead God's church today. We must likewise be willing to humble ourselves before God, and because of our concern to see people of all cultures come to follow Him, be willing to take essential steps that allow that to occur – even when it is uncomfortable for us.

Cross-Cultural Ministry Requires Discernment

In order to make certain that a church is reaching all persons in its community in a culturally relevant manner while remaining true to Scripture and at the same time not causing a great amount of dissension in the body takes discernment. It requires the discernment of leaders who are walking in close relationship with the Lord. God promises in James 1:5 that "If any of you lacks wisdom, he should ask God, who gives generously to all without finding fault, and it will be given to him." James goes on, however, to warn that "when he asks, he must believe and not doubt....That man should not think he will receive anything from the Lord" (James 1:6-7). The way to ask with confidence for God's wisdom and discernment is to make certain that we have a close walk with God, praying and listening to Him through His Word regularly. As Paul wrote to the Christians at Philippi:

And this is my prayer: that your love may abound more and more in knowledge and depth of insight, so that you may be able to discern what is best and may be pure and blameless until the day of Christ, filled with the fruit of righteousness that comes through Jesus Christ – to the glory and praise of God. (Philippians 1:9-11)

Richard R. Melick, Jr. writes that in this passage, Paul is calling for "the highest and best of Christian qualities and growth." Melick goes on to write that Paul is making the case that "failure to grow in the knowledge God expects hinders" the ability to discern God's will. On the other hand, growing under the leadership of the Holy Spirit allows us to discern God's will, which means knowing what "things are harmful and, therefore, should be avoided," but also the ability to affirm and embrace "the best of good choices." This discernment, according to Melick, is having "a wisdom related to life, ...the ability to discern moral conduct and values so that life and energy are not misdirected." He concludes that "a growing love, fed by proper knowledge and moral insight, enables one to see the best way to live..." (Melick, 65-6).

One area that needs to be discerned is exactly what changes a church needs to make to effectively reach out to persons of other cultures in its community. We will discuss in the next chapter some ways to discover what cultures are represented in a community, and how to learn about those cultures. This will certainly help in this decision.

A major part of determining if a change needs to be made is determining whether or not that change would be in tune with Scripture. We began this chapter with the truth that nothing we do as a church must put us in contradiction with God's Word. Many times this is easy to determine. But at times it may take God's wisdom and discernment to make a judgment.

Even if we conclude that a change would be useful and biblical, the timing in making the change needs to be settled on. This may take the greatest discernment of all. If we move too quickly, we may cause unnecessary conflict within the church that might not have occurred if we had we taken a bit longer to prepare the church for the change. On the other hand, if we wait until everyone is completely on board, we may never make the change. God's timing will always be perfect and church leaders need to be constantly seeking God's face as they lead their church through the process of becoming cross-cultural in its ministry.

Conclusion

These are some of the commitments that a leader must have and must lead his church to have if they are going to become involved in cross-cultural ministry that will lead to a multicultural church. This is certainly not an exhaustive list, but these are all biblically essential truths that must be accepted for a church to move successfully toward being multicultural without causing grave harm to the church body. Once the church and its leadership have made these commitments, they can move on to begin studying the community where the church serves to ascertain what cultural groups live there that will need to be ministered to. This will be the subject of the next chapter.

CHAPTER 3

PRACTICING CROSS-CULTURAL MINISTRY: RESEARCHING YOUR COMMUNITY

Introduction

Chapters 3 and 4 will build on the foundations of cross-cultural ministry that have been explained in the first two chapters, and will provide some tools for practicing cross-cultural ministry. If we believe that Scripture teaches that we should be reaching across cultures, then we must be obedient to put that into practice. As Jesus said to us in John 14:15: "'If you love me, you will obey what I command.'" The tools in these two chapters will help you obey the biblical teaching to reach out to all cultures.

In this chapter, we will discuss how to research a community. The purpose of such research is to understand the people in the community we serve, including the various cultures represented in the area. As we carry out this research, it will also helps us build better relationships with the people in the community. All of this is done because we want to better be able to minister and reach out to all persons in our community, no matter what their race or ethnicity.

We also research our community because it is biblical to do so. One example of this is Nehemiah. In the first chapter of the book of Nehemiah, he hears God's call to go to Jerusalem and help in the rebuilding of the city. As the second chapter of the book begins, Nehemiah becomes incarnational and moves to Jerusalem. He realizes he cannot minister from afar. When he reaches the city, we are told what he does first in Nehemiah 2:11-18:

> I went to Jerusalem, and after staying there three days I set out during the night with a few men. I had not told anyone what my God had put in my heart to do for Jerusalem. There were no mounts with me except the one I was riding on. By night I went out through the Valley Gate toward the Jackal Well and the Dung Gate, examining the walls of Jerusalem, which had been broken down, and its gates, which had been destroyed by fire. Then I moved on toward the Fountain Gate and the King's Pool, but there was not enough room for my mount to get through; so I went up the valley by night, examining the wall. Finally, I

turned back and reentered through the Valley Gate. The officials did not know where I had gone or what I was doing, because as yet I had said nothing to the Jews or the priests or nobles or officials or any others who would be doing the work. Then I said to them, "You see the trouble we are in: Jerusalem lies in ruins, and its gates have been burned with fire. Come, let us rebuild the wall of Jerusalem, and we will no longer be in disgrace." I also told them about the gracious hand of my God upon me and what the king had said to me. They replied, "Let us start rebuilding." So they began this good work.

We see in this passage that Nehemiah researched the community before he finalized his plans, shared it with others, and began the work.

This passage clearly teaches us that having a desire and even a willingness to work hard is not enough. It must be informed work. Mervin Breneman in his commentary on the book of Nehemiah puts it this way:

Nehemiah was to prove himself to be a hard worker. But hard work alone will not insure success. It must be the right work at the right time done in the right way. That takes planning. Praying and trusting God does not mean research is not necessary. Nehemiah wanted to assess the situation before presenting his project to the officials and the people. (Breneman, 179-80)

Jesus teaches the principle of the importance of planning before we begin a project in Luke 14:28-32:

> Suppose one of you wants to build a tower. Will he not first sit down and estimate the cost to see if he has enough money to complete it? For if he lays the foundation and is not able to finish it, everyone who sees it will ridicule him, saying, "This fellow began to build and was not able to finish." Or suppose a king is about to go to war against another king. Will he not first sit down and consider whether he is able with ten thousand men to oppose the one coming against him with twenty thousand? If he is not able, he will send a delegation while the other is still a long way off and will ask for terms of peace.

Jesus is speaking in this passage specifically about counting the cost of following Him before deciding to commit to do so (Stein, 396). But in making this point, He also offers the general principle of the foolishness of the person who does not research and plan before beginning an endeavor. This principle Jesus provides is certainly true for those who would desire to do cross-cultural ministry. The cost needs to be counted, the research and planning carried out carefully, and then the ministry can begin. Paul was practicing cross-cultural ministry – a Jewish man from Tarsus reaching out to Gentiles from many different cities of the world. He put Jesus' principle of researching first into practice in Acts 17:22-23:

> Paul then stood up in the meeting of the Areopagus and said: "Men of Athens! I see that in every way you are very religious. For as I walked around and looked carefully at your objects of worship, I even found an altar with this inscription: TO AN UNKNOWN GOD. Now what you worship as something unknown I am going to proclaim to you

If Paul had not first taken the time to examine the city of Athens and to know what was transpiring there, he might not have been ready for this encounter with the Greek philosophers and others who lived in that city. Because he knew something about the city, Paul was able to use the altars to other gods he had observed in the city to seek to make a point of contact with his listeners. He was able to attempt to use his knowledge of their city and culture to build a bridge from his biblical beliefs to their Greek philosophy and mythology (Polhill, 370-1). Paul understood the importance of first knowing the community you are seeking to minister to before beginning the ministry. We need to understand this as well and follow the examples that Scripture has given to us. The rest of this chapter will provide some tools for doing the necessary research.

Know Your Community

The first thing a church must do in any community is to learn who lives in that community. If we are going to minister to people, we have to know about them. One of the important things to learn is what cultures – what races and ethnicities – are represented in the community we serve. There are a number of ways to do this.

<u>Demographic Research</u>

One way to better understand a community is to study the demographics of the community. This is simply the study of the population of a community by looking for trends and movements within that population. Manuel Ortiz writes: "In order to assess the multiethnic situation in the United States, we need demographic information that we can utilize to formulate strategies for outreach" (Ortiz, 32). You especially want to look for changes in the makeup of the community in terms of racial and ethnic groups. This demographic information can come from a number of sources, including the following:

1. The United States Census Bureau can provide basic demographic material that can give us an overview of what is taking place in our community. It does an in-depth survey of all people living in the United States once every ten years. It also provides updated estimates every year in between the major censuses

using sample research. As the first strategic goal of their strategic plan states, they desire to "meet the needs of policymakers, business, non-profit organizations, and the public for current and benchmark measures of the U.S. population, economy, and governments." They go on to write: "Informed decisions require reliable, up-to-date information. The Census Bureau's programs give decision-makers current, timely updates on a wide range of subjects" (census.gov). This "wide range of subjects" includes the race and ethnicity of people living in various communities. Thus their information can be a good place to start. It will give a "snap shot" over-view of the community and let you know what races and ethnicities live there. It must not be the only information you depend on, however. Census Bureau information alone may not give an entirely accurate picture of your community. For example, many times, for a variety of reasons, people from other countries may not be counted. Therefore, you must turn to other sources as well.

2. City governments also often have informa-tion that can be helpful. Most cities have planning offices that can be especially helpful. Their purpose, as described by the planning department for one major city, is "to provide reliable information and advice to the City Manager, the City Council, other City officials, and the general public in order

to assist them in making sound decisions" (fortworthgov.org). They conduct research that specifically relates to the area in which your church is located. Therefore, they will almost always have more comprehensive and up to date demographic data than the United States Census Bureau has for your area. They will also do research looking at current and future trends that will include information far beyond what the Census Bureau provides.

3. Real estate agencies are another good source for information about who lives in and what is going on in a community. A good real estate agent or agency makes it a point to know about the communities that they are trying to sell in. This helps them to know how to market the homes they have for sale. Therefore, they can often tell you not only official information about the community that they have researched through official channels, but they can also provide informal information that they have gathered through their own personal observations and experiences while working in the community. This can be invaluable information for understanding the community your church serves.

4. Another source for both formal and informal information can be community groups. Many communities now have neighborhood associations that have been formed by people living in a particular community. I (David) live in a national historic district which has

a very active neighborhood association. The purpose of that association is to "improve the quality of life for all residents" in that neighborhood. As part of that goal, they seek to provide "useful information" so that people can "learn more about our neighborhood" (historicfairmount.com). When I served as Community minister at a church in this neighborhood, I found the neighborhood association to be a good source of official information about the community. They had done a great deal of research regarding such things as demographics as part of helping the city as it planned for the future of the community, as well as in order to apply for federal and private grants for community improvements. Not only did they have this type of official data, they had also done research in the area by surveying community residents. This provided more informal data that would never be found in demographic data. This is the type of information that neighborhood associations and other community based groups can provide when a church is trying to discover who lives in its circle of influence.

5. Local associations of churches can also have valuable information about the make-up of communities. Most major denominations have associations of local churches in a region that come together to support and encourage each other as they do the Lord's work in that area. Many areas also have groups made

up of churches of many denominations that work together in a similar way. These associations of churches can also be a rich source of information about the community. They often provide access to demographic data, many times data from sources other than the United States Census Bureau. I (Louis) am the pastor of a church in the greater New York City area. My church cooperates and I myself am deeply involved with a group of churches in that area known as the Metropolitan New York Baptist Association (MNYBA). I have found the MNYBA to be a valuable source of information for myself and my church as we have sought to minister in our community. Also, one of the reasons this book is being written is because of a need I observed in this association of churches of which I am a part. Because so many of the churches in this association are multi-cultural, and because so many different cultural and ethnic groups are represented in the Greater New York area where the Association's member churches are located, I determined that educating them about cross-cultural ministry, including cross-cultural communication would be an important step in helping them to (1) communicate better between themselves so they could work together more effectively, and (2) reach out to other persons in their community more productively.

Ethnographic Research

A second way to learn about the community your church serves, including what racial and ethnic groups are found there is to do ethnographic research. This is a term that is borrowed from the fields of anthropology and sociology. Ethnography is the study of a culture – its ideas, values, customs, patterns of behavior, food, dress, language, etc. The research is carried out from the point of view of both the researcher and the indigenous person, or the person from the culture being researched. The neighborhood is viewed as a new culture to be understood, including each culture, i.e., each racial and ethnic group represented in the community. The residents of that community are perceived as the "experts" who will teach the researcher. They are the ones who truly understand the community as a whole and the specific racial or ethnic group of which they are a part as well.

This is what we observe David do when he first becomes king over Israel. In 1 Chronicles 11, David is crowned after Saul's death. He conquers Jerusalem, moves into the city, and begins the process of restoring it. He did not seek to do this alone or with his own wisdom. 1 Chronicles 11:9 tells us that "David became more and more powerful because the LORD Almighty was with him." David certainly depended on God. But 1 Chronicles 11:8 also tells us that he worked with others. It states that David rebuilt one part of the city of Jerusalem, "while Joab restored the rest of the city." The rest of the 1 Chronicles

11 and all of 1 Chronicles 12 tell of all the people David brought together to help him restore and lead the city of Jerusalem and the nation of Israel. Rather than thinking that he could do the rebuilding of a city and nation all alone, he was wise and humble enough to seek the insight and help of others. One of the most interesting of those whom David learned from is found in 1 Chronicles 12:32, which describes "men of Issachar, who understood the times and knew what Israel should do." Commentary author J. A. Thompson writes about these men that they "had some skill in discerning the meaning" of what was happening in the community that was "resulting from shrewd observation" (Thompson, 127).

There are people just like this in the communities where we serve. We must find them and allow them to aid us in understanding the people we want to reach in the name of Jesus Christ. We must allow them to help our churches become more capable of ministering to the community where we are located, including understanding the different cultures represented there. This process requires what anthropologists and sociologists refer to as field work. This is being out in the community and interacting with the people who live there. It is getting out of the four walls of the church and moving beyond the comfortableness of demographics. There are many tools and methods that we must use to accomplish this task.

Observation

Observation is the first step of getting out into the community. The best way to do this is simply to go out and walk the streets of the community at different times to see what is going on. By walking the streets you can see things that you would never discover simply by looking at demographics about the community. By going at different times, you will see things from different perspectives. For example, if you walk by a park in the community where I (David) minister in the morning, you may see moms with their preschool children; if you walk by the same park in the late afternoon, you may see school age children running, riding bikes, and playing soccer; if you walk by that park on a Saturday afternoon, you will probably see large extended families celebrating one of their member's birthdays. If you did not go for your walks at different times, you would not learn these different facts. Thus by walking at different times, you can observe varying activities and meet different people, even though you walk the same route.

As you walk, you should be looking for various facts about the community. For example, you should look for the types of people who live in the community. What racial and ethnic groups do you observe? Does this match with what the demographics have shown? You should also be looking for what aged people seem to be most prevalent in the community. Do you see many children or evidence that children are around, i.e., bicycles, toys, etc? What types of housing do you see – single family, apartments, duplexes, single family homes turned into duplexes, etc. – and what condition does it appear to be in? Are the yards well kept? Are there houses being renovated, remodeled, and kept up in general, or are they being left to deteriorate? What community resources do you see? Are there many churches, community centers, parks, schools, etc.? What types of businesses are there? Are there grocery stores, for example, and if so, are they chain stores or local stores? Are there restaurants, and, again, if so, what types? Are the signs in the stores, restaurants, and other businesses in English, in a foreign language, or some combination of those?

All of these observations will help the church determine who lives in the community God has called them to serve. All of these observations will help the church develop a plan to better reach out to all persons in the community. These observations reveal truths about the community that only studying demographics would never reveal.

Participate in the Life of the Community

Not only do you want to be out walking the streets of the community, but you want to begin to get involved in activities that will allow you to learn more about the community, and to build relationships with people that will help you to better understand the community. There are many ways that this can happen.

One way to participate in the community is not just to walk past restaurants, businesses, etc. in the community, but to spend time there. Do your shopping in the local grocery stores and eat at local restaurants, for example. The types of food that are found in grocery stores or the types of restaurants that dominate in a community will help us greatly to ascertain the ethnic or racial makeup of a community. Eating at community restaurants regularly allows you to build relationships with the people that work there, which in turn allows you to learn more about the community from them, as well as possibly opening doors to ministry to them.

Another way of participating in a community is not only use the neighborhood association to gather information from, but to also join the association and become active in it. This is another way to get to know people in the community and build relationships with them. It is also a means to gain more informal information about the community as you work in the community on association projects such as neighborhood cleanups and neighborhood safety patrols, as you talk informally to people at meetings, or through an association newsletter.

These are just two ideas about how to more fully participate in the lives of people in your community. Each community is unique, and you will need to find out what organizations, events, businesses, etc. are available in your area that you can become involved in. It may be a parade, a tour of homes in the area, a neighborhood garden club, or any number of other activities that neighborhood groups would be glad to have more help with. Each one that you involve yourself in is another opportunity for you to better know your community and the people who live in it.

Talk to Community People

As you get to know people, you will be able to talk to them about the community. Some of these people you will get to know from your involvement in community activities and organizations. Some of them will be key persons who live and/or work in the community that can help you understand the community better. We have already mentioned real estate agents, for example, as persons who make it their business to know what is taking place in the community, especially in terms of who is moving in and out of it.

There are other key persons who also know what is taking place in the community. Principals of schools know especially about what is taking place among families in the community. They have responsibility to care for children in the community, but they also have regular contact with parents. When I (David) served on staff at an inner-city church, there was an elementary school right across the street from the church and another elementary school and a middle school just a few blocks away. The principals at these schools were more than happy to discuss the needs of the schools and the families of the children who attended there. They were glad to share their observations about the community and what was taking place within it. They were one of my best sources of insight about the community as our church sought ways to better reach out to the people that lived there.

Merchants and other business owners are also helpful in understanding trends in the community. Their livelihood depends on making certain they stay current with what is taking place in a community. If they do not, they will not know what to keep in stock or to produce to keep people coming and purchasing from them. There may also be social agencies and even other churches in your area, whose workers and ministers could help you get a picture of the people who live there.

Once again, each community is unique. You must determine what persons in your community would be key to talk to and take the time to do so. You will find that most of them will be glad to do so. As you talk to them, make certain you ask questions based on your own observations and research. This is a good way to confirm or dispel what you have come to believe is true about the neighborhood. Make certain you give them the opportunity to describe the trends they see taking place in the community. If you will be the learner and let them teach you, you will learn much from them about the neighborhood your church serves and the people who live there.

Build Relationships with People in the Community

While you will learn a great deal about the people in a community by looking at demographics, by getting involved in community events and organizations, and by talking to key people in the community, the information you gain will always be somewhat at a surface level. The only way to really know about the people in a community is begin to build relationships with them. This is especially true as we come across persons from different cultural backgrounds than our own. If we truly want to minister cross-culturally, then there comes a point when we must come to understand the other cultures represented in our community better. There is no substitute for doing this than by building relationships with persons from those cultures. We will talk more later in this chapter about understanding other cultures, but building relationships is the key. So as we study about and become involved in the community our churches serve, as we meet people from other cultures in that process, we must seek to build relationships with some of them in order to better understand them, in order that we can better minister to them in the name of Jesus Christ. We must move our relationships from what Edward T. Hall describes as "low" – where the relationship is official, status conscious, and formal – to what he refers to as a "high" relationship – where the behavior is warm, intimate, involved, and friendly. It is only through "high" relationships with persons from other cultures that we really come to understand them and their culture (Hall, 91).

Sherwood Lingenfelter argues that the book of Acts demonstrates that the building of relationships is absolutely essential for cross-cultural ministry. He points to Acts 2:44-47 as an example of this:

All the believers were together and had everything in common. Selling their possessions and goods, they gave to anyone as he had need. Every day they continued to meet together in the temple courts. They broke bread in their homes and ate together with glad and sincere hearts, praising God and enjoying the favor of all the people. And the Lord added to their number daily those who were being saved.

Lingenfelter comments that the lesson to be learned from this passage about cross-cultural ministry is:

That small collections of believers churches ... must be nurtured to form community through fellowship, prayer, eating together, and sharing basic resources.... Unless we help believers from a community, the sense of oneness in the body of Christ will not happen. Believers without the experience of the unity of the body of Christ may fall away.... (Lingenfelter 1992, 198)

Lingenfelter's point is that unless there are relationships built between believers of other cultures and ourselves, we will not be able to effectively minister to and disciple them so that they will grow into strong committed followers of Christ.

John Stott points out that this type of relationship building brings about what he refers to as "true dialog." He says that this is especially important since we want to present the Gospel to the other person eventually. This type of dialog not only allows us to build a relationship and understand better how to present the Gospel, but it also allows us to do so with integrity. We are not just viewing the other person as another prize won, but as someone we genuinely care about (Stott 1975, 71).

Stott writes that "true dialog" allows us to draw near to the other person. Our masks come down. We begin to be seen and known for what we really are. Mutual understanding is fostered as the conversation develops and deepens. We come to respect the other person's convictions, his culture, and to relate to his pain and struggles. We still want to communicate the good news to him, for we care deeply about being faithful to God's Word. Yet at the same time, we also care about the non- Christian with whom we want to share the gospel (Stott 1975, 72).

Second, Stott describes "true dialog" as a mark of humility. As we listen to others, our respect for them as human beings made in God's image grows. The gap brought about by differences in color of skin, accent and mannerisms diminishes. Third, he believes "true dialog" is a mark of integrity. We listen to our friend's real beliefs and problems. We also divest our minds of the false images we may have harbored about him and his culture. At the same time, we ourselves are determined to be real about our beliefs and problems. Fourth, Stott sees "true dialog" as a mark of sensitivity. He writes that Christianity and evangelism fall into disrepute when we attempt to evangelize by a fixed formula. The very essence of dialog, however, is an attempt at mutual listening. This makes it possible to react sensitively both to the actual needs of our friends and to the guidance of the Holy Spirit (Stott 1975, 73-4).

What are some ways we can go about building these types of relationships with persons from other cultures? One point that must be made first is that this must be intentional. Neither we nor the person we are seeking to get to know will desire to do this naturally. We talked in an earlier chapter about cross-cultural ministry being uncomfortable, especially at first. That it required us to purposefully move beyond our comfort zones. This is one of those places where that will be true. What are some ways we can intentionally reach out to and build relationships with persons from other cultures? There are a number of guidelines that can be helpful as we attempt to build these relationships:

1. Prayer is essential to all that we do. God calls us to: "Pray at all times in the Spirit, with all prayer and supplication" (Ephesians 6.18). Begin by praying that you will know how to be the other person's friend, and that they will know how to respond to your friendship and be your friend. You may find that you are feeling inadequate to the challenge. Never forget God's powerful presence in your life. God will equip you, but you must seek His help.

2. Study about the other person's culture before you meet with him. Discover basic things

like locating the persons' country on a map and reading about the educational and political systems, or the people and the country's current political situation. Be careful about talking about politics, however. Although you may disagree with the politics of his country, be very slow to criticize. You may not fully understand the situation as well as you think you do. Even if you do, you can accept each other as individuals. Learn about any dietary restrictions. For example, Muslims do not eat pork.

3. For the first contact, an informal visit or meal together is better than an elaborate dinner. Make certain you plan a meal that you know will not offend the person based upon dietary restrictions you learned about when studying his culture. Chicken and vegetables are usually acceptable to all.

4. Following up any verbal invitation with a written note is greatly appreciated by your guests. Always let the person know in advance about how long the visit or activity will last. Write down your name, address and phone number as well as the names of your family members for him.

5. Ask the other person to write down his name and the names of any of his family members who may be coming to dinner. Their names may seem impossible to pronounce, but if you will practice their full names until you can say them correctly, they will be pleased.

6. Host more than one person or family from the culture at a time. Ask the person if there are other persons they would like you to invite. Inviting more than one person or family at a time takes the pressure off any one person, and it makes him feel less alone. It also puts you and your family in the minority, which also helps make the other persons more comfortable.

7. When the persons are in your home for a meal, say it is your custom to give thanks for food and then say grace. After dinner, state that it is your custom to read a passage of Scripture, do so in a modern translation, make one or two comments about it, and then discuss any questions that may arise. This is not the time to preach a sermon. Then you may follow this with prayer, without singling out your new friends and praying for their conversion. However, it would be well to pray for them, that their work may be successful, and that their families may be preserved and blessed of God in every way.

8. During the first visit, make arrangements for when you will see them again. Tell them you enjoyed their visit. In making arrangements for the next visit, be specific about the date and time. You might even want to ask them to cook a meal for or with you that would be common to their culture.

9. Find out what hours they are available for phone calls. Get their phone number and

email address so you can communicate with them between visits. Tell them what hours you are available to be called. Try to be aware of their 'free' time and avoid visits when they are busy. Use the phone and e-mail to relay bits of news, future invitations or just to chat. This solidifies relationships. Your new friends will know they have not been forgotten.

10. As your relationship develops, you will want to move beyond just eating meals together. Some things you might want to do include:

   a. Invite your friend to participate in your normal daily routine activities: shopping, yard work, house cleaning, studying, and cooking, for example.

   b. Play a sport with him that is a favorite of his.

   c. Have a birthday party for your friend.

   d. Visit a museum, go to a play, or tour a parade of homes, and then discuss it afterwards.

   e. Participate in activities with their friends and their national group. This may include participating in activities that are part of the holidays they celebrate.

   f. Think of other activities you can do together or your families can do together that will build your relationship stronger and help you to learn more about his culture. (Selle, 18-26; Taussig, 116-24)

Communicating While We Build Relationships

While spending time with people from other cultures is important, it is also important that we know how to communicate with them as we spend that time with them. One thing that we need to remember is that we will make mistakes in our attempts to communicate with persons from other cultures. We must not let fear of making a mistake keep us from the attempt. We need to develop a good sense of humor and laugh with the other persons over our mistakes. We need to simply admit our faults and mistakes and seek their help in correcting them (Clement, et. al., 74). Then these mistakes become another way of learning. Remember that your purpose is to learn. So listen, be humble, and learn even from your mistakes. With that in mind, here are some guidelines for communicating with persons from other cultures as you seek to build relationships with them:

1. A smile is the same in any language. Warmth and sincerity bridge cultural gaps.
2. Friendships can best be developed through conversing.
3. Avoid idioms and colloquialisms. American jokes and humor are often misunderstood. Explain anything you feel might have been misinterpreted. Let your remarks be governed by sensitivity and good judgment.
4. Do not be afraid of difficulty in communication, either over the phone or in person. Friendliness and patience, combined with

genuine interest and understanding, will transcend language and other cultural barriers. When it is difficult to understand your new friend, do not give up. Speak slowly, write words down, practice patience, and listen carefully.

5. Asking "Do you understand?" or "What did you say?" too often may begin to undermine your friends' self – confidence. Speaking slowly and distinctly will aid them in understanding.

6. Do not pry into finances. Getting financially involved is usually unwise. Refer financial, legal or governmental matters to others.

7. Your new friends will be pleased to teach you greetings in their language. Learn how to say *hello, good-by, welcome* and special greetings for significant days of celebration in their countries. In return, tell them about *Merry Christmas, Happy New Year* and other greetings.

8. Be patient if time does not mean the same to your friends as it does to you. Theirs may not be a time-controlled culture like American culture is. Discuss time differences and expectations.

9. Be a good listener, as it opens the way for a deeper friendship.

10. Encourage your new friends to talk about themselves, their families, and their countries.

11. Do not always be asking questions about them. Share a little about yourself, your family and your work.
12. Ask what family games they play, what holidays they observe, and how they are observed.
13. Learn from them about their professions and goals.
14. Listen to tapes of music they like. Ask them to bring tapes or CDs of music they like or that is representative of their culture.
15. Ask to see their photo albums of their families. Learn the names of members of their families. (Selle, 18-26; Taussig, 116-24)

Building these types of relationships with persons of other cultures is extremely important. It is not only important to our church as it seeks to minister in its community, but it is important to us personally, to the people we are building the relationship with, and most importantly to God, who loves them deeply. As Carl Selle writes:

It is important to recognize that we are also enriched by this friendship. Not only do we have the opportunity to appreciate and gain first-hand information about the geography, politics, history, customs, culture and religions of world countries, we also can serve fellow human beings who are experiencing loneliness, culture shock, or physical need. (Selle, 18)

What We Want to Learn

As we study demographics about the community our church ministers in, as we observe this community while walking its streets, involving ourselves in its activities, and talking to its citizens, and as we build relationships with persons who live in that community, especially those from cultures different than our own, what are we looking for? What are we hoping to learn? There are a number of answers to that question.

Trends

As we gather all of this information, we want to first of all look for trends that we observe about the community that might help us better minister to the people there. This would include in a general sense, such areas as the age of the people in the community. Does it seem to be aging or getting younger? Many communities that are attracting persons from other races and ethnicities than the white Anglo culture tend to be getting younger. There tend to be more families with small children. Another factor that can be important to a church is the socioeconomic condition of persons in the community. Is the people's income tending to go upward or downward? Of course, knowing these factors can help a church develop ministries to reach persons in the community.

But this book focuses on cross-cultural ministry. So the trends we want to look for in this area are racial/ethnic trends. We want to look to see what racial and ethnic groups are represented in the community we serve and how many of each group are represented. This will help us to know what other cultures we may need to focus on as we try to reach out to everyone in our community. We will want to begin by focusing on those groups that have the largest representation in our community.

Another thing we want to look at is what racial/ethnic groups are growing in number. This can help us plan for the future as well as the present. There is a sociological theory that can be useful to us at this point. It is called the tipping theory. This theory states that:

> As the population of a particular ethnic group builds up to a visible presence in an area, it reaches a tipping point triggering its transformation into an ethno-community. When this occurs, households of other ethnic backgrounds filter out, and the demand for the neighborhood's housing stock largely comes from the infiltrating ethnic group. (Qadeer, 19)

There has been no set percentage determined that an ethnic or racial group must grow to that will guarantee that the community is going to "tip" at that point. Some studies have shown that even a small fraction of the presence of a racial or ethnic group in a white community can cause that community to "tip" from a predominately white community to a predominantly ethnic or racial community (Easterly,

2). One study found that it took as high as thirty two percent of a community changing to a particular racial or ethnic group for it to "tip" in favor of that group (Ellen).

Though a specific percentage may not be able to be determined that leads to a community "tipping," the theory is viewed as being inevitable and universal. It is viewed by most sociologists and anthropologists as an irreversible and systematic process. The determining factor regarding the point at which a community tips is racial attitudes. The predominant racial or ethnic group will only remain as long as the new group remains at a percentage that the current predominant group can tolerate. Once the currently predominant group begins to anticipate that they may lose control of the decision making power in the community, the community will "tip" (Ellen).

One interesting insight that research studies on this tipping theory have found is that white communities seem to "tip" more quickly than other racial or ethnic communities. While no group likes to be in a very small minority, other racial and ethnic groups seem to be less sensitive to racial/ethnic composition than white persons. It has been demonstrated through research that this is because white persons tend to have more negative perceptions about what a neighborhood made up predominately of persons of a non-white background would be like. Specifically, they tend to view such communities as low income, having little power in the city as a whole, and, therefore, having deteriorating school quality, public safety, and property values (Ellen). This is certainly a view that churches must help their members to overcome if they are going to remain in a changing community and to minister effectively there.

Organizations in a community can use this idea of the tipping theory to help in planning for the future. If they see a community "tipping" in a certain direction, they can plan accordingly. Mohammed A. Qadeer describes how this occurs:

> The concentration of an ethnic group facilitates the development of religious, cultural, and community institutions. A building with a sizable number of Muslim tenants, for example, allows pooling of funds to rent a room for daily prayers, or in the case of Chinese Christians, to provide services in Cantonese. Additionally, public schools, community centers, and health services can offer programs for women, the elderly, or children which are specifically tailored to their linguistic and social needs. Ethnic groceries, restaurants, and video stores also often emerge, thereby rounding off the process of institutional completeness in the community. (Qadeer, 19-20)

Churches can learn from this and plan for their futures in their communities as well.

Worldview

Another aspect of our communities and the new cultures that are moving into them that can be ascertained by our research is worldview. Every cultural group has a worldview, which is a set of more or less systematized beliefs and values which that group uses to evaluate and attach meaning to the reality that surrounds it. World view is not separate from culture. It is included in culture as the deepest level presuppositions that a cultural group has, and it is on the basis of these that people in that group live their lives and structure their actions (Kraft, 97, 115). Thus by understanding the worldview, we not only understand the behavior of persons, but we understand the values behind the behavior.

By studying a culture's worldview, we discover their norms. These norms are the ways that are "normal" for that culture when it comes to living life. It is their way of life; their way of behaving as dictated by the set rules and regulations of their culture. It is the sum total of all the expectations, values, and aspirations of any given culture. Discovering these norms is absolutely essential to reaching out to another culture. If we do not understand them, we cannot build a lasting relationship with people of another culture. When we understand these norms, then we can adapt our way of doing ministry (not the essentials of the message) so that we can build bridges to persons of the other culture. When we adapt to the other person's culture, we are opening a wide door for ourselves right into the very heart of the people we want to reach out to. We are then able to convey to them by our own example of selfless love the extent of God's love for them (Clement, et. al., 74-5, 96, 163).

As we saw previously in this chapter, Paul understood the importance of understanding worldview as a way of building bridges to persons of other cultures so he could share the gospel with them. A prime example of this was his ministry to the Athenians in Acts 17. We too as the modern church must understand and accept the importance of understanding worldview. What are some examples of norms that we should understand so we can better build bridges to another culture?

Child Rearing

How a culture raises and trains its children is very important to understand (Clement, et. al., 163). For example, the Mexican-American home is usually very child-centered. The child is cherished, pampered, and thoroughly "spoiled." He is regarded as an *angelito* because he is seen as not yet contaminated by human error. He receives adoring affection from both mother and father. Parents also tend to be permissive, especially with the male, who is overindulged, allowed to be loud and aggressive; he is accorded greater status than females (DeGenova, 67; Madsen, 51; Queen, et. al., 305). We may find that our methods are very different, but we must be careful not to be critical of how other cultures go about this process unless it directly contradicts Scripture.

A major aspect of child rearing that is vital to understand are the rites of passage that are important to a culture and how that culture celebrates these. Rites of passage are the rituals carried out to mark different stages of development in a person's life as he passes from childhood to adulthood (Clement, et. al., 163). This can be a great point of contact with a culture. An example of this, once again from the Mexican-American culture, is the *quinceanera*. This is the celebration of the fifteenth birthday of the female, which marks her coming of age as a young woman. It is celebrated by a mass or prayer service that includes a sermon in which the young woman is reminded of her future responsibilities as a wife and mother (DeGenova, 68).

Customs

Every culture has customs that are unique to them. It is crucial that we come to understand these so that we can adapt our way of doing things to theirs. One good example of this is the greeting. Persons from a Japanese culture bow when they greet another person, while Americans generally shake hands. Therefore, bowing is a feature of Japanese culture, while the handshake is a feature of American culture (Blommaert, 17). If we as Americans recognize this, then when we are ministering cross-culturally to Japanese persons, we can adapt our way of greeting.

Another example of the need to adapt our greeting is when Americans greet each other with "Hi! How are you?" When they do this, they are seldom out to seek medical, social or psychological information from their friends. Nor are they necessarily conveying concern for a friends' welfare. It is usually nothing more than a casual greeting. A person from another culture, unaware of this social convention, may be put off by such behavior. One annoyed Indonesian graduate student, for example, said of an American: "He asked 'How are you?' and then walked away before I could tell him how I was feeling!" This almost impersonal practice was mistaken by the Indonesian student for a warm greeting, a cue to stand around and chat (Lau, 61).

Time

Americans take time very seriously. They consider being on time to be a virtue and thus a norm, and to be late to be a faux pas. For example, if a movie does not start on time, an American audience may soon stomp, yell, and hiss as people express anger about the delay. While the American culture is a time oriented one, this is not true of all cultural groups. Latin American and Yapese cultures, for example, are more event oriented. People who are time oriented express great concern about punctuality, the length of time expended, and utilization of time to its maximum potential. People who are event oriented show concern that an activity be completed regardless of the length of time required, and emphasize unscheduled participation rather than carefully structured activities. Thus in the Latin American culture, a person is excused for being late up to one-half hour, tension over being late begins to develop at about one hour late, and people become hostile about how late a person is at about two hours. In the Yapese culture, there is even greater grace when it comes to lateness. Lateness is excused for up to two hours, tension occurs at about three hours, and hostility begins at about four hours late. An American would never tolerate either of these, generally. They will only excuse lateness for about five minutes, tension develops at about fifteen minutes, and hostility begins at about one-half hour (Lingenfelter and Mayers, 39, 44). We must discover which view of time the culture we are seeking to reach out to has, and if it is different from ours, be willing to adapt accordingly.

Sherwood G. Lingenfelter and Marvin K. Mayers provide the following table to help us understand better some of the basic differences between time oriented and event oriented cultural views:

Table 1
Time and Event Orientations

Time Orientation	Event Orientation
1. Concern for punctuality and amount of time expended.	1. Concern for details of the event, regardless of the time required.
2. Careful allocation of time to achieve the maximum within set limits.	2. Exhaustive consideration of a problem until it is removed.

3. Tightly sched-
   uled, goal-directed
   activities

4. Rewards offered as
   incentives for effi-
   cient use of time.

5. Emphasis on dates
   and history.

3. A "let come what
   may" outlook not
   tied to any precise
   schedule.

4. Stress on completing
   the event as a reward
   in itself.

5. Emphasis on present
   experience rather
   than the past or
   future.

(Lingenfelter and Mayers, 41)

Understanding another culture's view of time, especially regarding what it means to be considered late to an activity, is crucial for building bridges to people from that culture. Lingenfelter and Mayers write the following about the importance of this view of time:

An important key to effective cross-cultural ministry is an incarnational attitude toward time and event – we must adapt to the time and event priorities of the people with whom we work. When we Americans enter other cultures, however, we often bring a cultural blindness to this issue. We feel the urgency of time and orient our lives to reflect our own culture. God commands us, however, to do nothing out of self-centeredness but to consider others better than ourselves (Phil. 2:3-5). Our attitude should be the same as that of Christ Jesus, to satisfy the time and event priorities of others before considering our own. With such a goal, we will move toward a more effective ministry to persons whose cultural values are different from our own. (Lingenfelter and Mayers, 50)

When it comes to the concept of time, we who come from a time oriented culture must remember what William McConnell states when he writes that time is "a gift from God, and that his priorities can always be fulfilled in the amount of time we have been given... God is lavish with his gifts, so that there is always enough time to do what Jesus calls us to do" (McConnell, 89).

The important thing is not that everything is done according to our time but that they are done according to God's desires. It is His desire, as we have already established, that all people from all cultures be reached with the Gospel of Jesus Christ. In order to do this, we must deal with differences in views about time so that we can effectively build bridges to people from other cultures.

Communication Style

Cultures vary greatly in the way they communicate. Of course, language is of utmost importance. If there is a difference in language, unless one of the persons from different cultures is willing to learn the other's language, there will be very little communication taking place. But even when speaking the same language, communication style differences between two persons from differing cultures can be so in opposition to one another that building a bridge between the two becomes nearly impossible. What are some key ideas about communication that we must look for that we must be willing to address if we want to minister cross-culturally?

First is the idea of formality. Americans tend to be very casual and informal in both social and professional interactions. Many other cultures find this type of informality, especially in all situations and with people who are strangers, to be unacceptable (peacecorps.gov).

Second is non-verbal communication. An American is taught to look a person in the eye to show self-confidence, as well as respect for the other person and interest in what he is saying. However, many Asian cultures consider looking someone straight in the eyes while conversing with him to be rude and to show a lack of respect (peacecorps.gov).

Third is directness of presenting ideas and responding to others' ideas. Americans say what they mean. There is not much need to read between the lines. "Telling it like it is," or, in other words, complete honesty, even if it means hurting someone else's feelings or pride is considered of great value. This is not the case in many other cultures. In other cultures, people are often indirect. They imply or suggest what they mean. It is expected that a listener will read between the lines. Understatement is valued. If the truth is going to hurt someone, it should not be stated, or it should at least be tempered. Many Asian cultures regard highly what has come to be known as the concept of "face." In fact, it might even be said to be paramount. You try by all means and if at all possible to save someone's reputation, to not embarrass him. Maintaining harmony is the overriding goal. Thus confrontation is avoided at all cost. It is very difficult for someone from a culture where face is highly valued to say "no" to someone, or to correct even the most obvious of mistakes made by another person. They may even find it difficult to tell you they do not understand what you are saying, for they believe this would show you disrespect and might offend you by telling you that you were not communicating clearly enough (peacecorps.gov).

Fourth is personal space. Americans are very jealous of their space. They do not like people to come too close to them while they are conversing. They also do not appreciate a lot of touching. People from some cultures like to be very close, almost face to face, with the person they are talking to. Touching, hugging, etc. is a very important part of communication in many cultures.

Food

Food is very important to cultures. Being willing to learn what persons in another culture eat and being willing to eat what they like is crucial to building bridges to them. The Bible speaks to the importance of this on several occasions. In the first chapter of this book, we looked carefully at how God taught Peter the importance of being willing to eat what the Gentiles eat so that he could minister to them (Acts 10). We also discussed how when Peter struggled with this idea later on that Paul had to confront him and remind him of the importance of being willing to eat cross-culturally (Galatians 2:11-13).

Paul further demonstrated the importance of what we eat in 1 Corinthians 8 when he wrote about eating meat offered to idols. He wrote there:

> Now about food sacrificed to idols: We know that we all possess knowledge. Knowledge puffs up, but love builds up. The man who thinks he knows something does not yet know as he ought to know. But the man who loves God is known by God. So then, about eating food sacrificed to idols: We know that an idol is nothing at all in the world and that there is no God but one. For even if there are so-called gods, whether in heaven or on earth (as indeed there are many "gods" and many "lords"), yet for us there is but one God, the Father, from whom all things came and for whom we live; and there is but one Lord, Jesus Christ, through whom all things came and through whom we live. But not everyone knows this. Some people are still so accustomed to idols that when they eat such food they think of it as having been sacrificed to an idol, and since their conscience is weak, it is defiled. But food does not bring us near

to God; we are no worse if we do not eat, and no better if we do. Be careful, however, that the exercise of your freedom does not become a stumbling block to the weak. For if anyone with a weak conscience sees you who have this knowledge eating in an idol's temple, won't he be emboldened to eat what has been sacrificed to idols? So this weak brother, for whom Christ died, is destroyed by your knowledge. When you sin against your brothers in this way and wound their weak conscience, you sin against Christ. Therefore, if what I eat causes my brother to fall into sin, I will never eat meat again, so that I will not cause him to fall. (1 Corinthians 8:1-13)

In this case, Paul is not specifically speaking about another culture, but he does speak about why we should be concerned about food as we relate to other people. Paul states that it really does not matter what we eat, but it may matter to someone else with whom we are eating. And if we insist on our "rights" of eating what we want, it might cause someone to stumble in their walk with Christ, in the specific instance Paul refers to here (Mare, 240), or in the case of cross-cultural ministry, cause someone to stumble in coming to Christ in the first place.

Paul concludes his discussion of this topic by writing in 1 Corinthians 10:31-33:

So whether you eat or drink or whatever you do, do it all for the glory of God. Do not cause anyone to stumble, whether Jews, Greeks or the church of God— even as I try to please everybody in every way. For I am not seeking my own good but the good of many, so that they may be saved.

Here he makes clear that while food may not be important to us, it is of the utmost importance to others. Even if we have trouble understanding that, we must remember that ultimately it is not the other person that should be in view at all times, but God. His glory must always be our objective in everything we do as Christians. Paul is saying:

That doing all for the glory of God means thinking of the good of others, both Christians and non-Christians (v.32). The mention of Jews and Greeks may refer to the unsaved groups talked about in 1 Corinthians 1…. So we find encompassed by these verses the two great commandments – love God and love your neighbor (Matt 22:37-39). Paul seeks to benefit others, not himself. His ultimate objective in all his conduct is that people might be saved – not superficially but fully to the glory of God. (Mare, 253)

This must also be our ultimate objective, and if it takes eating food we may not like, then we need to follow Paul's lead and think of God and His kingdom and not ourselves.

Conclusion

This chapter has presented some ideas for researching a community so that we can discover who resides there. In America's ever diversifying cities and towns, this will almost certainly include people from different cultures than your own. Once that is discovered, it becomes necessary to learn more about the people you have discovered so you can better minister to them. We have presented just a few of the important aspects to seek to learn about people from other cultures than your own. While this is not an exhaustive list, it will put you well on your way to understanding the other culture better, and to reaching out to them. In the next chapter, we will take the final step and show you how to use the data you have collected and the information you have learned, and put it into practice to help your church minister cross-culturally. We will also discuss some of the key aspects of leading in a multicultural church – how to respond to challenges that are certain to arise as you bring people from other cultures into your midst.

CHAPTER 4

PRACTICING CROSS-CULTURAL MINISTRY: TURNING RESEARCH INTO RESULTS

Introduction

We discussed in Chapter 3 how to research a community to discover who lives in it, including what different racial and ethnic groups are represented there. This chapter will discuss how to take what you discover about the community and use it to help your church reach all persons there. Specifically, we will look at key issues in doing multi-cultural ministry. We will first look at some ideas that can help you and your church become more welcoming to persons from different cultures. Next we will look at how to deal with some of the challenges that will arise as a church seeks to minister cross-culturally, such as leadership, communication, and conflict resolution. We conclude the chapter by considering how to reach out to one very important and growing population in the United States that requires cross-cultural ministry – international students.

Preparing a Church to Be Cross-Cultural

In an earlier chapter, we made the point that cross-cultural ministry is intentional. This is because it goes against our natural inclinations. Therefore, there are some steps that a church must take if they discover that there are persons from other cultures in their community, and they want to reach out to persons in that different culture. We will begin this chapter by offering some suggestions for helping a church to become better able to minister cross-culturally.

1. First, the church as a whole must recognize that the community is changing and that the church needs to change in response to the changing environment and demographic. Individual church leaders, such as the pastor, may realize that the community is changing and believe that a response is necessary. That is why they have done the work to research the community. But in order for the church to meet the needs of the community where it ministers, the entire congregation (or at least a strong majority) must be committed to look for new direction from God.

2. Next, the church needs to completely assess the situation. They need to take the data gained in the research to see what the significance is for the church. They must ask questions such as: Is the community headed toward permanent change in racial and/or ethnic makeup? What will the community look like in five or ten years? What resources does the church have in place that can be used to respond to the changing community at this time? What resources need to be added to continue to respond to the needs of the people in the future as the community continues to change? This assessment should be led by the church leaders, but the entire congregation should be involved in the process.

3. Recasting the vision of the church is the next thing the congregation must do. The church should meet to pray and reflect in an attempt to discover the relationship between the data gathered, the assessment and the resources they possess as a congregation. Out of this should come the development of a mission statement that will assist the church in its focus to do ministry that is effectual in the context of a multiethnic community. It should include in written form the biblical position of the church on the matter of unity in diversity. Involve multiethnic leaders in the process by bringing in Christian leaders from the racial or ethnic background of the people in the community you want to reach to serve

as consultants and experts to help in your planning.

4. Put the vision and mission statement into action. Begin with small steps or "pilot programs," that allow the church to put the vision into practice with a greater chance for success, while allowing the members of the congregation to gain a better understanding of the other cultures they will be ministering to. This will give the church members confidence and enthusiasm about expanding their efforts to reach out to persons from other cultures (Ortiz, 135-7; Pocock and Henriques, 198-9).

5. Before the mission statement is put into action, there needs to be a time of commitment to the task. A service should be held in which the new vision and mission statement of the church are presented. The biblical justification should be given by the pastor and other leaders, and the church as a whole should be challenged to publicly make the commitment to joyfully accept the new vision. Remember that crossing cultures is a difficult thing, and if there is not a commitment to the task, discouragement will soon set in and the task will be replaced with the comfort of reverting back to old ways.

   a. The people must be challenged to admit and confess any ethnocentric and prejudicial thoughts and feelings they may have. They must be warned that these could arise again, and that every time they do, they must be taken captive as ungodly and turned over to God for His help in overcoming them. As Paul writes in 2 Corinthians 10:5: "We demolish arguments and every pretension that sets itself up against the knowledge of God, and we take captive every thought to make it obedient to Christ." We must believe that as we do this, God will transform us by the renewing of our minds, as Paul writes about in Romans 12:1-2: "Therefore, I urge you, brothers, in view of God's mercy, to offer your bodies as living sacrifices, holy and pleasing to God—this is your spiritual act of worship. Do not conform any longer to the pattern of this world, but be transformed by the renewing of your mind. Then you will be able to test and approve what God's will is—his good, pleasing and perfect will." We must ask God to replace ethnocentricity and prejudice with His love. As Paul states in Romans 5:5: "And hope does not disappoint us, because God has poured out his love into our hearts by the Holy Spirit, whom he has given us. (Grunlan and Mayers, 26).

b. The church members must be challenged to and asked to commit to respect and esteem the other culture they are about to seek to minister to. They must be reminded that there will be aspects of the culture they will not like. They must also be challenged to remember that the Bible, not their personal preferences, is the criteria by which all cultures, including their own must be evaluated.

c. Church members must be warned that this will be a painful task. It might cause them to lose some of their identity with their own culture. Others in their culture may not understand why or even like that they are reaching out to persons from other cultures. At the same time, they will never fully be part of the new culture. In a sense they will be part of a new culture – what Paul Hiebert calls a bridge culture. Hiebert makes the point that bridges are stepped on, which is painful (Hiebert, 227). But it will be a worthwhile sacrifice, for across that bridge will cross the Gospel message.

d. The congregation must be challenged that in the midst of their unsettled feelings and the painfulness of the process of implementing the new vision, they must keep their focus on the primary task - to bring people of all cultures to a relationship with Jesus and under the authority of His Word.

6. Some things the church as a whole needs to do early in the process of reaching out include:

a. Just as the leadership and perhaps a few others in the church did in the research phase, the entire church needs to become involved in building relationships with people in the community from the culture you are trying to reach out to. They need to be able to talk with persons from that culture and learn from them. You may have to help set up these relationship building opportunities. Perhaps a first step might be a fellowship with members from another church that has members from the culture you are trying to reach, if such a resource is available in your area. As they build these relationships with people from other cultures, church members will develop empathy for the other culture. This will lead to a greater desire to minister to persons from that culture.

b. People in the church as a whole need to study the new culture your church is trying to reach. Training sessions about this culture would be appropriate. A leader from the other culture could lead these sessions. He could be invited to preach at the church as well.

c. The church members must train the people to be sensitive to and to accept other cultures. They must be asked to make a commitment to this, and then they must be helped to do so through training.

7. As the church moves beyond these initial baby steps and begins to grow in its desire to reach persons from the another culture, and as the church begins to actually reach some people from that new cultural background, it will want to expand the steps it is taking to be more attractive to persons from the other culture. The church will attract some new, committed Christians to be a part of its membership. But if it wants to continue to attract new people and to retain those it has already attracted, the church will need to continue to change. What are some things the church can do to become all the more appealing to persons from the new culture it is trying to reach?

    a. The church must make its worship contextualized. It must make its worship represent the new culture as well as the old. This is one area that the previous church members will have to be willing to compromise on. Many may have to overcome strong ethnocentric feelings at this point. What does this include?

        -   Music must represent the new culture as well as the old. Music is very important to cultures, and so if a church is serious about reaching out to a new culture, that new culture's music must be represented in its worship.

        -   Typically, worship must be more participatory. People from many cultures enjoy being a part of the worship service in various ways rather than simply sitting and watching or just being entertained.

- Persons from the other culture should be included on the platform. They can read Scripture, pray, sing solos or be part of music groups, and can be involved in any other ways you can think of.

- The pastor will need to change his sermon and pastoral prayers to make certain they reflect concerns and illustrations that represent the new culture as well as the old.

b. The new culture will need to be represented in church leadership. This means both volunteer leadership positions and paid staff positions. This will help increase the presence of the other culture on the platform as mentioned above, but it will also show that the church is serious about considering persons from the new culture as equal in God's eyes. This will require a willingness on the part of persons from the old culture to submit to leadership of other cultures. This is another area that will challenge the members of the church from the old culture.

c. The church will need to develop a wholistic mentality and ministry. Ministry to many cultures will mean going beyond the "typical" activities that churches become involved in, i.e., worship services, Bible studies, visitation, etc. It will have to expand to new areas like providing job training, teaching English as a Second Language classes, learning to navigate immigration laws, etc. The church will have to be open to discovering and meeting needs represented among the people of the culture they are trying to reach.

8. Evaluation will need to constantly be taking place. Any new initiative needs ongoing refinement. This will especially be true for such a radical change as will be taking place in a church that is truly becoming multicultural. You will need to constantly determine what changes are taking place in the community. You will need to constantly be determining how to respond to those changes and other needs that arise within the congregation itself as it evolves.

9. Prayer must be an ongoing part of this endeavor. While this was saved for last, it is certainly not least. Only God will provide the wisdom to know how to best reach across cultures. Only God will change the hearts of people so that they will desire to do this, and only He will keep them on track. Therefore, it is essential that this entire process be constantly bathed in prayer.

Manuel Ortiz suggests that there is one key area that a church will need to be aware of as it moves itself toward becoming a church that reaches out to new cultures and is becoming multicultural. Such a church, he contends, must be deliberate in determining how to resolve conflicts (Ortiz, 137). Conflicts will surely arise in any church. Bring people together from different cultural backgrounds and those conflicts are both more certain to arise and to be more pronounced. Therefore, we will now focus on some tools to help leaders and their churches respond to the changing needs of a changing church. This should in turn help the church avoid some conflict, and be better able to navigate through the rough waters of conflict when it does come.

Cross-Cultural Ministry and Transformational Leadership Strategies

The intention of this section is to guide leaders in learning how to transform their leadership strategy to become more culturally sensitive in a multicultural community, as well as how to become a more vibrant and effective leader in general. The leader will be the key to making cross-cultural ministry and a multicultural church work. Therefore, this section is dedicated to helping the church leader alter his style to be more productive in his new and changing environment.

The word transformation means "to change the nature, function, or condition of; to convert" (Webster's, 1170). Once a sinner comes to repentance and joins the church, he is a transformed person, able to walk in the newness of life. In order to be effective in relating to all cultures, the pastor needs to transform his ministry into innovative strategies, as opposed to the traditional ones he may be accustomed to. He needs to be aware of today's climate. We do not live in a modern society, but a postmodern one. In short, "postmodernism means a negation of modernism" (Goetz, 52). If the Gospel is to reach out to this present generation within a multicultural community, then certain methods need to change, or the ministry will die.

Ray A. Seilhamer states: "The church needs transformational leadership. If you always do what you've always done, you will always get what you have always got" (Seilhamer, 66). The end result of this merry-go-round strategy is the death of the church, nothing more, and nothing less. Lyle Schaller explains in the magazine, *New Results*, the difference between a transactional leader and a transformational leader. He introduced this theme with a testimony from a layperson. "You want to know why this church changed from growing older and smaller to growing younger and larger? I'll tell you. Our new minister is a real leader and that has made all the difference in the world" (Schaller).

Seilheimer explains that: "A transformational leader is driven by a vision of a new tomorrow and wins supporters and followers for that vision which will transform the congregation" (Seilhamer, 67). Leith Anderson, in the book, *Dying for Change*, adds insight to that description when he states: "A leader is one who knows the road, who can keep ahead, and who can pull others after him" (Anderson, 188). Seilhamer adds to our understanding of what is needed in a leader as he writes:

> The transformational leader takes initiatives. Leaders are realists that are open to new ways of thinking. They are the creators of new paradigms. Transformational leaders excel amid adversity. Jesus, a transformational leader, faced constant turmoil. Conflict is a major epidemic in the contemporary church, which centers on tradition, personality, power, control, ritual, and mission. We need leaders in the church that will not run from conflict but who understand principles of conflict management and resolution. (Seilhamer, 68)

Seilhamer makes the point that because transformational leaders are breaking with tradition and leading their churches into new areas of ministry, conflict will occur. Therefore, they need to be skilled at dealing with conflict. Cross-cultural ministry is transformational, and conflict as the transformation is carried out is inevitable.

Conflict is often the result of communication problems, and those problems are accentuated when crossing cultures. Communication is always filtered by such things as worldview, learning, experiences, beliefs and attitudes. Differences in any of these can alter the message between the sender and the receiver (Thomas and Brewster). When we communicate with someone from the same culture, there is a likelihood that many of these filtering elements will be similar. But when we communicate with persons from other cultures, there is a high probability that many or even all of these filters will differ, thus leading to miscommunication and conflict. One of the tasks of the leader of a church involved in cross-cultural ministry is to set the example for the rest of the congregation by seeking to improve his cross-cultural and conflict resolution skills. As John Gargner states: "Leaders must go to the root of communication breakdown whether it is anger, fear, mistrust, or different definitions" (Gargner, 12).

How then does a leader set the example and communicate effectively with persons from other cultures? It must begin with the leader's willingness to serve others, to be a servant leader who is willing to patiently learn the filters of the other culture for the sake of better communication that can lead to better ministry and better communication of the Gospel. Robert K. Greenleaf describes this aspect of leading in his book entitled, *Servant Leadership*: "Servant-leadership emphasizes increased service to others;" it promotes "a sense of community, and sharing of power in decision making" (Greenleaf, 16). A leader or pastor needs to humble himself and surrender his personal pride to the total ministry of the church.

Counter-Culture Leadership

There are a number of characteristics that are necessary if a leader is to practice the type of servant leadership that will allow him to be transformational and thus minister effectively in a multi-cultural organization. They are characteristics that will lead to better communication and less conflict. Seilheimer calls this type of leadership counter – culture leadership because it goes against the typical type of leadership proffered in American culture as effective. These strategies would be helpful to any leader, but they are especially needed by the minister in a multi-cultural setting where the challenges are greater in number and concentration. The following principles are helpful in discovering a counter-culture leadership perspective (Seilhamer, 71-74):

1. Leadership must be confirmed. A leader cannot simply proclaim himself a leader. Others must confirm that they see God's hand at work in his life, that he exemplifies the characteristics of biblical leadership, and that he is a mature and growing person who has the skills to lead others to do likewise. God confirmed Jesus' ministry from its beginning through John the Baptist, who said of Him in John 1:29-34:

   The next day John saw Jesus coming toward him and said, "Look, the Lamb of God, who takes away the sin of the world! This is the one I meant when I said, 'A man who comes after me has surpassed me because he was before me.' I myself did not know him, but the reason I came baptizing with water was that he might be revealed to Israel." Then John gave this testimony: "I saw the Spirit come down from heaven as a dove and remain on him. I would not have known him, except that the one who sent me to baptize with water told me, 'The man on whom you see the Spirit come down and remain is he who will baptize with the Holy Spirit.' I have seen and I testify that this is the Son of God."

God further confirmed Jesus' ministry at His baptism in Matthew 3:16-17:

As soon as Jesus was baptized, he went up out of the water. At that moment heaven was opened, and he saw the Spirit of God descending like a dove and lighting on him. And a voice from heaven said, "This is my Son, whom I love; with him I am well pleased."

2. Leaders pray to God. They realize that they need God's wisdom and power to deal with the challenges that come with cross-cultural ministry. Nehemiah, an Old Testament leader with excellent leadership qualities, demonstrated his dependence upon God through prayer in Nehemiah 1:4-11:

When I heard these things, I sat down and wept. For some days I mourned and fasted and prayed before the God of heaven. Then I said: "O LORD, God of heaven, the great and awesome God, who keeps his covenant of love with those who love him and obey his commands, let your ear be attentive and your eyes open to hear the prayer your servant is praying before you day and night for your servants, the people of Israel. I confess the sins we Israelites, including myself and my father's house, have committed against you. We have acted very wickedly toward you. We have not obeyed the commands, decrees and laws you gave your servant Moses. Remember the instruction you gave your servant Moses, saying, 'If you are unfaithful, I will scatter you among the nations, but if you return to me and obey my commands, then even if your exiled people are at the farthest horizon, I will gather them from there and bring them to the place I have chosen as a dwelling for my Name.' They are your servants and your people, whom you redeemed by your great strength and your mighty hand. O Lord, let your ear be attentive to the prayer of this your servant and to the prayer of your servants who delight in revering your name. Give your servant success today by granting him favor in the presence of this man." I was cupbearer to the king.

3. Leaders know and understand people. They take the time to study the culture of the people they are reaching out to and to build relation-ships with them that allow them to better understand how to cross over to them. Jesus said, "I am the good Shepherd; I know my sheep and my sheep know me" (John 10:15).

4. Leaders invest in people. They understand that people are our human resources and

that they need to invest in their education, their spiritual growth, and their intellectual development, as well as provide new experiences designed for growth of people. Paul showed this type of investment as he spoke to the leaders in Ephesus in Acts 20:18-21, 26-27, 31:

When they arrived, he said to them: "You know how I lived the whole time I was with you, from the first day I came into the province of Asia. I served the Lord with great humility and with tears, although I was severely tested by the plots of the Jews. You know that I have not hesitated to preach anything that would be helpful to you but have taught you publicly and from house to house. I have declared to both Jews and Greeks that they must turn to God in repentance and have faith in our Lord Jesus...Therefore, I declare to you today that I am innocent of the blood of all men. For I have not hesitated to proclaim to you the whole will of God...So be on your guard! Remember that for three years I never stopped warning each of you night and day with tears.

5. Leaders have the courage to confront. When they see persons in their church who are not living by God's standard, including His love for all people of all cultures, he cares enough about those persons to confront them with the truth of God's Word. He does not allow their relationship with God or the church's mission

to be jeopardized because he does not want to take the chance of hurting someone's feelings. Jesus was a confrontational leader. He confronted Nicodemus about his spiritual life in John 3:3: "In reply Jesus declared, 'I tell you the truth, no one can see the kingdom of God unless he is born again.'" He confronted the woman at the well in John 4:17-18: "'I have no husband,' she replied. Jesus said to her, 'You are right when you say you have no husband. The fact is, you have had five husbands, and the man you now have is not your husband. What you have just said is quite true.'"

6. Leaders break with tradition. Leaders hear new ideas and try new things. They are not bound by prejudice and stereotypes; they keep the creative juices flowing. Jesus was often condemned for breaking traditions of the church in His day, as in Mark 7:1-5:

The Pharisees and some of the teachers of the law who had come from Jerusalem gathered around Jesus and saw some of his disciples eating food with hands that were "unclean," that is, unwashed. (The Pharisees and all the Jews do not eat unless they give their hands a ceremonial washing, holding to the tradition of the elders. When they come from the marketplace they do not eat unless they wash. And they observe many other traditions, such as the washing of cups, pitchers and kettles.) So the Pharisees and teachers of the law asked Jesus, "Why don't your disciples live according to the tradition of the elders instead of eating their food with 'unclean' hands?"

7. Leaders are visionary. They do not simply take what others have done and try to copy it. They seek to lead the church to discover what God wants to do uniquely with them where He has planted them. George Barna, author of the *Power of Vision*, speaks of one form of this when he writes: "Vision is conceptual, but it is also practical and detailed. If a vision for the individual churches is mandated from the denominational level, it assumes that the pastor of a church is not a leader but a manager" (Barna, 49). We see examples of God's vision being the basis of a leader's direction thoughout Scripture. One example is Paul being led to carry the Gospel message to Macedonia in Acts 16:9-12:

During the night Paul had a vision of a man of Macedonia standing and begging him, "Come over to Macedonia and help us." After Paul had seen the vision, we got ready at once to leave for Macedonia, concluding that God had called us to preach the gospel to them. From Troas we put out to sea and sailed straight for Samothrace, and the next day on to Neapolis. From there we traveled to Philippi, a Roman colony and the leading city of that district of Macedonia. And we stayed there several days.

8. Leaders help others discern the vision. This process of discernment involves both listening and seeing. Effective leaders are good listeners; they listen to their constituents and their fellow workers. Effective leaders are also great visionaries who rely on foresight, hindsight, depth perception, peripheral vision, and revision (Ortiz, 135). A leader should also focus on God's agenda. Leighton Ford puts it this way: "Our vision must come from the same place as Jesus'. It must come from the Word of God and from Spirit-filled minds and imaginations, and from asking, "How does Jesus see my world?" ... Our task is not to develop strategies, but to see Jesus' vision and understand what the Father's strategy is for our lives" (Ford, 23). Leaders need to involve the congregation in writing out their vision statement. Christian Breuninger indicates that vision must be clearly articulated, compelling, grounded in reality, and must be repeatable (Breuninger, 19). Aubrey Malphurs adds that: "Vision must challenge people; it is a mental picture; it concerns the future; a good vision is feasible and must have a sense of urgency" (Malphurs, 92). As we can see from the Acts 16 passage quoted in point 7 above, Paul was able to pass his vision on to the rest of his missionary team, for Luke writes in verse 10: "After Paul had seen the vision, we got ready at once to leave

for Macedonia, concluding that God had called us to preach the gospel to them."

9. Leaders embed core values. Core values can be defined as the consistent, passionate core beliefs that drive the ministry's vision. Core values are important because they communicate what is important, what really matters. We can observe from the quotation from Acts 20 in point 4 above that Paul embedded the core values of God's Word into the church at Ephesus, for as he says, "for three years I never stopped warning each of you night and day with tears" (Acts 20:31). And what was it that he warned them with? The word for "warn" used here is *neutheteo* and it literally means "to put into the mind of" (Zodhiates, 1017). So what had Paul put into their minds for three years? Acts 20:27 tells us, where he states: "I have not hesitated to proclaim to you the whole will of God." The list of values should be short but comprehensive; brief enough so our values can be embedded into our daily deeds and comprehensive enough to measure how well we do what we propose (Malphurs, 92). The interpersonal and group dynamics that characterize the leader's relationship with other key leaders is where this embedding of core values into the culture of the organization most powerfully takes shape. Schein states that this imbedding of core values allows the church to maintain its focus on its mission (Schein, 93). There

162

are three tasks necessary to maintain internal integration and thereby create an organizational culture according to Schein:

a. The first task is to create a common language. Creating common conceptual categories and a shared language are important functions of the leader because those common, abstract words like "seeker," "worship," and "community" need concrete definitions to support the articulated assumptions of the church culture.

b. The second task is to define group boundaries. This task entails answering important questions like: Who is in? Who is out? What will be the requirements for membership? For leadership? How will the expectations differ for those who only attend Sunday worship? How will we assimilate people into the life of our church, and what will this process communicate about our values?

c. A third task involves the distribution of power. This is best accomplished by a team based ministry led by a coach whose primary role is defined as equipping servants in a positive way (Schein, 93). In addition to these tasks, Schein suggests that leaders embed culture by how they react to critical incidents, how they allocate scarce resources, and how they select, recruit, and promote others.

Schein calls these "embedding mechanisms" (Schein, 383).

10. Leaders create leaders. Christ was a disciple maker who created leaders to carry out His work once He was gone from the earth. His approach to discipling was a four-step process: I will do it, you watch me; I will do it, you help me; you do it, I will watch you; you do it, someone else will watch you (Gargner, 12). We see this from the beginning of Jesus' time with His disciples. After instructing them for a while, Jesus then sent them out to do ministry because He was training them to be the future leaders of the church. We read about this in Luke 9:1-6:

When Jesus had called the Twelve together, he gave them power and authority to drive out all demons and to cure diseases, and he sent them out to preach the kingdom of God and to heal the sick. He told them: "Take nothing for the journey—no staff, no bag, no bread, no money, no extra tunic. Whatever house you enter, stay there until you leave that town. If people do not welcome you, shake the dust off your feet when you leave their town, as a testimony against them." So they set out and went from village to village, preaching the gospel and healing people everywhere.

Jesus later said to His disciples just before He went to the cross:

When the Counselor comes, whom I will send to you from the Father, the Spirit of truth who goes out from the Father, he will testify about me. And you also must testify, for you have been with me from the beginning" (John 15:26-27).

11. Leaders are role models. A primary responsibility of leaders is to recognize that they are role models of how others should behave. "Every action that a leader takes, or doesn't take, is information about the leader's values and seriousness about those values" (Nanus and Bennis, 109). Paul saw himself as a role model as he writes about in Philippians 3:17: "Join with others in following my example, brothers, and take note of those who live according to the pattern we gave you."

12. Leaders are architects of organizational structure. "A thoughtful, flexible infrastructure coordinates efforts, gives direction to the vision, and frees the leader from 'hands on' involvement in areas outside his or her giftedness and calling" (Beckhard and Pritchard, 2). Organization structure is never an end in itself; it is a means to a vision-driven mission (Breuninger, 21). Moses developed this type of structure with the help of his father-in-law to lead God's people from Egypt to the Promised Land. We see this in Exodus 18:13- 26:

The next day Moses took his seat to serve as judge for the people, and they stood around him from morning till evening. When his father-in-law saw all that Moses was doing for the people, he said, "What is this you are doing for the people? Why do you alone sit as judge, while all these people stand around you from morning till evening?" Moses answered him, "Because the people come to me to seek God's will. Whenever they have a dispute, it is brought to me, and I decide between the parties and inform them of God's decrees and laws." Moses' father-in-law replied, "What you are doing is not good. You and these people who come to you will only wear yourselves out. The work is too heavy for you; you cannot handle it alone. Listen now to me and I will give you some advice, and may God be with you. You must be the people's representative before God and bring their disputes to him. Teach them the decrees and laws, and show them the way to live and the duties they are to perform. But select capable men from all the people—men who fear God, trustworthy men who hate dishonest gain—and appoint them as officials over thousands, hundreds, fifties and tens. Have them serve as judges for the people at all times, but have them bring every difficult case to you; the simple cases they can decide themselves. That will make your load lighter, because they will share it with you. If you do this and God so commands, you will be able to stand the strain, and all these people will go home satisfied." Moses

listened to his father-in-law and did everything he said. He chose capable men from all
Israel and made them leaders of the people,
officials over thousands, hundreds, fifties and
tens. They served as judges for the people
at all times. The difficult cases they brought
to Moses, but the simple ones they decided
themselves.

13. Leaders are ready to respond when cultures
clash. These other principles will help alle-
viate conflict, but it will not prevent it.
Conflict is inevitable, because if leaders are
serious about reaching out to new cultural
groups, they will be calling for change, and
change brings conflict. Negotiating conflict
also involves a focused affirmation of the
agreed values of the congregation and a flexible orientation toward the implementation of
the vision (Breuninger, 18). A clear purpose,
vision, and a mission statement will help
to counter conflict. We looked in an earlier
chapter at Paul's response to Peter when
the Gentile and Jewish cultures clashed in
Galatians 2:11-12:

When Peter came to Antioch, I opposed
him to his face, because he was clearly in the
wrong. Before certain men came from James,
he used to eat with the Gentiles. But when
they arrived, he began to draw back and separate himself from the Gentiles because he was
afraid of those who belonged to the circumcision group.

Clearly Paul had no problem responding to this clash of cultures.

Crossing Over

These characteristics of a servant or counter-culture leader open the door for him to become a transformational leader; one who is ready to lead his church to reach out to persons of other cultures. But if he is truly going to lead his church toward cross-cultural ministry, he must be willing to learn all he can about the culture he is seeking to minister to. In order to do this, he must cross over to another culture; he must learn as much as possible about and become involved in the new culture he wants to lead his church to reach. Crossing over to another culture and then returning to one's own enables the leader to re-evaluate his ministry approach for effectiveness.

David Augsburger has well said about cultural sensitivity in doing ministry: "A theology that functions on the boundary requires a commitment to presence, to dialogue, to crossing over and coming back between worlds" (Augsburger, 36). John Dunne helps us further understand the importance of crossing over when he writes:

> What seems to be occurring is a phenomenon we might call "passing over," passing over from one culture to another, from one way of life to another.... Passing over is a shifting of standpoint, a going over to the standpoint of another culture, another way of life .... It

is followed by an equal and opposite process we might call "coming back," coming back with new insight to one's own culture, one's own way of life…. (Dunne, 9-10)

This two way pilgrimage across boundaries has great benefits according to Clasper. He comments:

To " pass over" is to enter a new world; to "come back" is to return a different person. One is bound to look at one's own world with fresh eyes and with fresh questions once the journey of friendship has been taken. It is easy to see why a narrow, fearful sect-mentality always urges a careful restriction of personal contacts. One can be "contaminated" by alien perspectives! Friendships are risky and threatening adventures. They can draw us out of our isolation and our restricted worlds. They force new concerns, new questions, and new priorities upon us. If we want to "remain the same" it is best not to venture out in significant friendships. (Clasper, 125-7)

Crossing over to another culture and returning to his own enables the pastor to be more effective in ministry. To do effective ministry one needs to consider contextualization of the total ministry of the church. It is a part of the transformation process. Such crossing over allows the leader to better understand the new culture to help in this contextualization of worship, leadership style, etc. that is so important in ministering cross-culturally as we discussed earlier in this chapter.

Contextualization

Cross-cultural ministry requires contextualization of the church's message and ministry. Therefore, the pastor must be able to know what this means and how to do it. He must teach his other leaders and the whole church about it as well. According to Hesselgrave and Rommen, contextualization is both verbal and nonverbal and impacts theologizing; Bible translation, interpretation, and application; incarnational life style; evangelism; Christian instruction; church planting and growth; church organization; worship style – indeed all of these activities are involved in carrying out the Great Commission (Hesselgrave and Rommen, 200).

In his book, *Anthropological Insights for Missionaries*, Paul G. Hiebert describes the following theological foundations that are critical if one wants to do contextualization without compromise of God's truth:

First, the Bible is taken as the final and definitive authority for Christian beliefs and practices. Second, the priesthood of the believers assumes that all the faithful have the Holy Spirit to guide them in the understanding and application of the Scriptures to their own lives. Third, there is the constant check of the church. Contextualization of the gospel is ultimately the task not of individuals and leaders, but of the church as a discerning community. (Hiebert, 191-2)

Contextualization is particularly important if we want to effectively communicate the gospel message to all cultures. David J. Hesselgrave in his book, *Planting Churches Cross-Culturally,* suggests that: "By gathering information on how the target community feels about the Christian message, the gospel communicator will be aided in contextualizing that message and putting biblical teaching into language the audience can understand." He adds that "once we have identified and characterized our target audience, it is natural to ask how we will communicate the (contextualized) message to them. The key to successful gospel communication is to utilize as much variety as possible" (Hesselgrave, 163-4).

Hesselgrave and Rommen, suggest seven areas that we must look at to understand how best to contextualize our message and ministry:

1. Worldview, which is the other culture's ways of viewing the world, as we discussed earlier in the book.
2. Cognitive processes, which is how that culture thinks through things. We will look at an example of this later in the chapter when we discuss ways that different cultures respond to crises that arise.
3. Linguistic forms, which are ways the culture uses to express ideas.

4. Behavioral patterns, which are set ways of acting in varying situations based on the culture's teaching.

5. Communication media, which is how the culture channels the messages it needs to get to its members.

6. Social structures, which is how members of the culture interact with one another.

7. Motivational sources, which are the ways that the culture makes decisions, and then how its members are encouraged to carry out those decisions. (Hesselgrave and Rommen, 203)

When it comes specifically to looking for ways to tell the Gospel message to the other culture, Hesselgrave suggests the following questions to ask to help contextualize that message:

1. At what points are the hearers most likely to misunderstand the gospel?

2. Which of the religious beliefs held by the audience are similar to the Christian world-view and can thus be expected to provide conceptual bridges for communication? Which are decidedly different?

3. To what special concerns of the target audience does Christ speak with authority and clarity?

4. What adaptations have successful Christian communicators used in addressing this or similar audiences? (Hesselgrave, 164)

On the subject of contextualization, Augsburger writes "Every piece of behavior and every belief must be considered in 'the framework within which' it takes place. This includes the premises, the surrounding standards, the overarching worldviews - what is beneath, around, and above the item or event" (Augsburger, 69-70). It is imperative that contextualization of Biblical truth be accomplished, for apart from this a cross-cultural ministry effort will most likely not be productive. But by contextualizing the Biblical truth we will be more productive and can do greater ministry.

Cross-Cultural Conflict Resolution

As we mentioned earlier in this chapter, conflict is a major part of and a major hindrance to doing cross-cultural ministry and to developing multicultural churches. Therefore, a leader who desires to minister across cultures, must be able to deal with conflict, especially that which is unique to cross-cultural ministry. Duane Elmer states it like this: "A healthy approach to understanding and managing conflict is a good beginning to cross-culture relationships" (Elmer, 34). As we also mentioned earlier in this book, nothing allows us to understand another culture better so that we can contextualize our ministry and message than building relationships with members of another culture so that we can dialogue with them. While such dialogue helps us to contextualize, it also helps us to respond to conflict. Dialogue offers a new way of dealing with the conflicts that inter-racial and multi-cultural differences bring. It allows our own ethnocentrism, nationalism, and traditionalism to come to the surface. These are a major cause of conflict between cultures. We who would seek to minister to another culture must be the ones who take the initiative and discover where we need to change. Here are some ways we can respond to some of the hindrances to our own successful involvement in cross-cultural ministry:

1. Ethnocentrism – As Christians, we should first understand our own ethnocentrism. Second, we should understand that specific cultural expressions are important to the person of the other culture that God brings across our path. We should adopt Paul's intercultural relationship as found in 1 Corinthians 9:19-23 that we looked at quite extensively in Chapter 1.

2. Nationalism –We need to affirm Biblical values first and foremost, and be willing to evaluate and even criticize our own culture's values. We must remember that our first citizenship is in and loyalty is to God's kingdom. As Paul, himself a proud Roman citizen, wrote in Philippians 3:20: "But our citizenship is in heaven. And we eagerly await a Savior from there, the Lord Jesus Christ."

3. Traditionalism – While being strong proponents of our tradition, we must be stronger proponents of doing what it takes to bring the Good News message to those who have yet to believe in Christ, no matter what their

language or ethnic group. This means remembering that traditions are not usually biblical, and, therefore, can be laid aside if it helps in reaching out to another culture. We must not be guilty of the Pharisees' sin of making their traditions more important than obeying God's Word and ministering to people. We see this as Jesus confronts the Pharisees in Matthew 15:3-6:

Jesus replied, "And why do you break the command of God for the sake of your tradition? For God said, 'Honor your father and mother' and 'Anyone who curses his father or mother must be put to death.' But you say that if a man says to his father or mother, 'Whatever help you might otherwise have received from me is a gift devoted to God,' he is not to 'honor his father' with it. Thus you nullify the word of God for the sake of your tradition."

We see this again in Matthew 23:1-4:

Then Jesus said to the crowds and to his disciples: "The teachers of the law and the Pharisees sit in Moses' seat. So you must obey them and do everything they tell you. But do not do what they do, for they do not practice what they preach. They tie up heavy loads and put them on men's shoulders, but they themselves are not willing to lift a finger to move them.

Instead of judging other cultures, it is wise to dialogue and find command ground with them so that we can reach out to them with the Gospel. Patty Lane asserts: "Different cultures have fundamentally different ways of valuing relationships, community, time, authority and many other aspects of life" (Lane, 47). Therefore, to understand each other in a better way, we should take time to dialogue with other cultures. Eric H. F. Law affirms that: "We must be willing to open our ears to listen, our minds to reflect, our lips to dialogue and our hearts to change if we are to continue to address diversity constructively" (Law, 354).

Daune Elmer gives us the example of some common principles we will probably discover and need to consider when dealing with persons from Two-Thirds World countries as follows:

1. The degree to which shame, face and honor are core cultural values will determine how important it is to choose an indirect method to communicate with the person, especially when correction is needed.
2. If the other person has had extensive exposure to Western culture, sensitive directness may be acceptable, understood and not offensive.
3. All forms of confrontation should occur in private, if possible, so as to minimize any loss of face.
4. Understand the various indirect methods used in the Two-Thirds World, and be alert to which ones are used and under what circumstances.

5. Ask God for help in understanding and applying unfamiliar conflict resolution strategies.
6. Scripture is the final judge of all cultural forms; prayer and discussion may be required before some cultural expressions are embraced. (Elmer, 181)

These principles are worth considering when dealing with conflict in a multicultural ministry. Although we live in America, if we came from another country, we do not think like Americans; therefore, each conflict needs to be considered case by case in its own context.

Cross-Cultural Crisis Management

Conflict often leads to crises, so the leader involved in cross-cultural ministry must also be skilled at responding to crises. While individuals in any culture may tend to fall into one of two types of crisis response, individual cultures do seem to produce a typical response among its membership. The two types of crisis responses that people tend to fall into are:

1. Noncrisis-oriented persons who have an abundance of optimism and believe that anything can be overcome, any challenge handled, and everything can be done with the present resources. They ignore both potential

and real problems and often refuse to seek advice from others.

2. The crisis-oriented persons, on the other hand, shake their heads in dismay at the lack of predictability that the crisis represents. Crises arise with startling frequency, and the crisis-oriented individual rebels at the lack of preparation for and the unpredictability of the situation. These individuals in conflict begin to question the spiritual commitment of others as the stress of the situation takes its toll on their emotional and physical well-being. They see no way that the situation can ever be overcome. (Lingenfelter and Mayers, 71)

Table 2 helps show some other differences in these two types of approaches to a crisis situation.

Table 2
Crisis and Noncrisis Orientations

Crisis Orientation	Noncrisis Orientation
1. Anticipates crisis	1. Downplays possibility of crisis
2. Emphasizes planning for crisis	2. Focus on actual experience
3. Seeks quick resolution to avoid ambiguity	3. Avoids taking action; delays decisions

4. Repeatedly follows a single authoritative, preplanned procedure

4. Seeks ad hoc solutions from multiple available options

5. Seeks expert advice

5. Distrusts expert advice

(Lingenfelter and Mayers, 71)

The challenge for the Christian leader is to understand how others will likely respond in a crisis situation, so that he can be better prepared to minister to that person when a crisis does arise. The leader himself must have an unwavering declarative commitment to the gospel and an open, questioning, combination of crisis and noncrisis-oriented lifestyle and ministry. He must have a biblical orientation, which means taking the best from both of the described orientations. Paul charges Timothy: "Be prepared in season and out of season; correct, rebuke and encourage with great patience and careful instruction" (2 Timothy 4:2). The command to be prepared suggests that a crisis orientation is needed so that the servant is ready for preaching and teaching opportunities, whereas the instruction to serve "with great patience" suggests a noncrisis orientation in personal life and ministry to others (Lingenfelter and Mayers, 71-76).

Sharing the Gospel Cross-Culturally

One of the main reasons we want to purposefully reach out to persons of other cultures is so that we can share the Good News of what God has offered us in Jesus Christ. Practicing the things we have been discussing in this book will give us the best opportunity to do this. There are some specific strategies that will help us use the tools we have been discussing in this book to speak the Gospel to persons from cultures different than our own:

1. Pray for God's love to shine through you. The Holy Spirit is the real agent of change. God's love speaking through the power of the Holy Spirit will impact people. A person can outwit your logic, but they have no answer for your love and the Holy Spirit's drawing. Prayer will bring these elements into the equation.

2. Work along family lines wherever possible. Most cultures place a heavy emphasis on family. Work through the heads of families or key decision makers. In many cultures, if this person comes to Christ, he will lead the other members to Christ as well. We observe this often in Scripture, for example, the jailer that Paul preached the Gospel to in Acts 16:27-34:

   The jailer woke up, and when he saw the prison doors open, he drew his sword and was about to kill himself because he thought the prisoners had escaped. But Paul shouted,

"Don't harm yourself! We are all here!" The jailer called for lights, rushed in and fell trembling before Paul and Silas. He then brought them out and asked, "Sirs, what must I do to be saved?" They replied, "Believe in the Lord Jesus, and you will be saved—you and your household." Then they spoke the word of the Lord to him and to all the others in his house. At that hour of the night the jailer took them and washed their wounds; then immediately he and all his family were baptized. The jailer brought them into his house and set a meal before them; he was filled with joy because he had come to believe in God—he and his whole family.

3. Avoid confrontation wherever possible. Understanding the other person's culture and adapting your style of delivering the message will help in this area immensely.

4. Discover what they know. What do they already know about the Bible and the story of Jesus and salvation?

5. Find the common ground. We discussed Paul's visit to Athens in Acts 17 earlier in this book. Just as he used an element from their culture to make a connection for the presentation of the Gospel, we may be able to do likewise. Again, understanding as much as possible about the other person's culture will help us in this.

6. Identify their burning questions and felt needs. The Bible addresses people's needs. If we can

show them that, it makes God's Word come alive with relevance for them, and they will be much more open to other truths from it.

7. Use Bible illustrations and redemptive analogies. These are usually much easier to communicate across cultures.

8. Study their response and clarify misunderstandings. Be patient. A response will not likely come quickly. Be willing to continue to dialogue with the person, answer their questions, and keep praying for him. Remember that it is not your job to bring the person to Christ. That is the role of the Holy Spirit. Our role is to faithfully and patiently present the message in the most culturally relevant way. (Grunlan and Mayers, 117-9; Guffey, 1)

Lawson Lau suggests another aspect of presenting the Gospel cross-culturally when he writes that: "Attention has been centered mainly on imparting the gospel at a personal level. Another approach is to expose our friends to the public proclamation of the gospel" (Lau, 90). Lau then goes on to suggest some steps to take to utilize public proclamation as a way of presenting the Gospel to persons of other cultures:

1. Invite the person to hear the Gospel preached at church or some other public event. "Most people are prepared to do almost anything once. For non-Christians this includes going to a church service. Having said this, it is

nevertheless helpful not to invite our friends merely to a 'church service.' It is better to invite them to hear a specific talk given by a particular person in a church."

2. Find out if the person has ever attended a church service before. If they have not, we will need to explain what they can expect.

3. If there is a coffee or fellowship time after the service, we should also remain with the person rather than wander off to visit with other Christians. Try to create an atmosphere of warmth. Introduce the person to your friends at church and to the person who spoke, especially if it is the pastor of the church. Our actions are a significant part of our witness to persons.

4. A follow-up step we could take is to discuss the experience. The discussion will help us to gain some insights into the person's spiritual state. "Do they perceive any relevance in the message? Is there any attempt at personal application? We could also try to correct any misconceptions they may have. Or we may perceive that they are ready to commit their lives to Christ. We should then encourage them to make this life-transforming decision." We should always be open and ready to explain clearly how the person can be saved. (Lau, 90-92)

Ministry to International Students: An Example of Cross-Cultural Ministry

Now that we have completed providing some insights about how to minister to a culture different than your own, we will look at one example of doing so. As we discussed in Chapter 1, the United States is becoming ever more multicultural. One area where this is occurring is in our nation's colleges and universities. If you have such a school near you, you can almost be certain that you can have an opportunity to minister cross-culturally. This section of the chapter will focus on a few ideas about how to do this.

<u>Where to Make Contact with International Students</u>

If you have made a commitment to reach international students through hospitality and building a friendship with them, the next decision is to discover exactly where to look. As we have stated, international students are found at almost every major university, community college, English-language institute, etc., especially in major metropolitan areas, but even in smaller communities. Major universities and four-year colleges will not only have large numbers of foreign students, they will also have special offices or centers on campus and several full-time staff members to coordinate activities. The person in charge is usually referred to as the "foreign student advisor" and is the appropriate person to contact for information. These schools will often offer volunteer

opportunities where you are welcomed to participate. Airport pickup, emergency housing, host families, English conversation assistance, international
dinners, and household goods exchanges are areas
where you might be willing to serve (Selle, 18).

My (David's) church has had an agreement for
several years with a major university in our city. We
contacted the school's international student office and
were told that there was an opportunity to provide
host families for a group of Chinese businessmen who
come to the university to spend two years furthering
their education. One of the areas these Chinese businessmen want to improve on is their conversational
English. Therefore, a number of our church members
gained training in teaching English as a Second
Language (ESL). We have also now become one of
the major sites that the university sends people for
ESL training – not just the Chinese businessmen, but
other international students as well. This arrangement
has given our church a tremendous opportunity to
build relationships with these folks, and many have
heard the Gospel. A few have even prayed to receive
Christ, and then returned to their homes as believers.
What a great mission opportunity.

Ministering to International Students

Once you have found the students, it is time to
begin to minister to them. Of course, as should be
clear from this chapter and the last, the place to begin
is by seeking ways to build relationships with them.

Here are some specific ways that this can be done with international students:

1. Ask members of your church to adopt a student or family. Building relationships with one person or family is much easier than trying to minister to the entire contingent as a group.

2. Commit yourself to develop real communication and understanding with your "adoptee." This assumes a profound respect for, genuine acceptance of, and growing knowledge about other persons and their background, work, hopes, and general situation of life. It requires your willingness to ask questions, listen, learn, and to be open to and "present" with your new friend. Try to understand the religious beliefs and cultural practices of your new friend. Remember that your friendship is a unique learning experience for both of you.

3. You must be careful not to behave in a patronizing manner. You must not give the impression that you are just doing your international friend a favor. You want to try to do things with them, not for them. If they want to do things for you, such as cook you a meal, you must be willing to accept this as another opportunity to learn.

4. You must be careful not to fall into the ethnocentric, thinking everything American is automatically best attitude. This might cause you

to look down on everything foreign, including different aspects of your new friend's culture. You must not think that because something is different, like eating with chopsticks instead of a knife and fork, it is inferior. This kind of superior attitude creates more resentment among internationals than anything else. At the same time, you must be willing to admit some deficiencies in your own culture and way of life, and you must receive criticism graciously. This will show humility to the other person that will help him open up.

5. Discover ways you can be of service to your new friend. They may need transportation, help finding housing, help finding work, or just basic information about life in America.

6. Discover how you can cooperate with the university or college. Learn from those administrators, faculty, counselors, and others who work with foreign students. Find out what services – admissions, language opportunities, academic counseling, international offerings in the curriculum, etc. – are available for your international friend.

7. Discover what organizations on campus work with international students. Look especially for Christian organizations. Find out what opportunities they offer; try to learn from and cooperate with them. While your friendship will be important, it is also important that they develop friendships with other internationals, especially others from their home-

land. They can understand what your friend is going through better than you can.

8. Invite the student to dinner at your home. There is no better way to build relationships than in the casual atmosphere of a home and over a meal. Cook a "typical" meal from your culture.

9. Find things you can do with the student that are "typically" American. International students are generally eager to understand Americans and the American way of life. Even commonly held ideas and familiar customs are new to most international students and their families. Do simple things such as: go fishing or hiking; bake cookies; fly a kite; decorate a Christmas tree; color eggs at Easter; share a Thanksgiving dinner; go caroling; or celebrate a holiday from your friend's country; visit a historic or scenic site; take a camping trip; enjoy a farm or a factory; just take a drive in the country.

10. Christmas can be an especially important time. Almost all international students know about and are curious about this holiday. Invite them to spend Christmas at your home. Christmas provides an obvious occasion to talk of Christ. Christians in their home can easily show the Christ of Christmas to their new friends. It may be enlightening to ask what Christmas means to your guest. The atmosphere of a home renders it an ideal environment to talk of that which is close to

your heart, including the real meaning of the holiday.

11. Invite your friend to special events at church such as Easter or Christmas services. Musicals are especially good events to take advantage of, for music is an aspect of culture most people are interested in, including international students.

12. There are two "nevers" to remember as you minister to international students:
    a. Never abandon your new friend. He will experience culture shock, loneliness, fear, and a longing for home. He needs you to stand firm as he goes through these things. He needs to know he can count on you. Find time to listen and care.
    b. Never terminate the relationship. Even if they do not seem to warm up to your witness, do not give up. Be sure God is using the friendship in some way.

13. There are also two "always" we need to remember:
    a. Always pray for your friend. Trust that God hears and answers prayer.
    b. Always be looking for opportunities to share the Good News of Jesus Christ with your friend.(Guffey, 1; Jordan; Little, 7; Selle, 18-26)

If we will put these strategies into practice, God will use us in the lives of international students. He will use us to bring the message He has for all people

– that He loves us and showed us that love ultimately in His Son Jesus Christ. His love will shine through us, and our new friends will believe that our words are real to us because they will see evidence of it in our lives.

I (Louis) can speak about this from personal experience. Since I came to the United States as an International Student, I recall right from my college days how having an international ministry in the college helped me to connect with Christian friends. I was privileged to attend international student camps organized by International Students Ministries, where I met students from other countries who were attending other colleges and universities. Besides good fellowship, good food, and activities like a talent show, there were also many attractive seminars presented to benefit international students in the camp. The camp was open to all the international students regardless of their religion and ethnicity.

During my seminary days, I recall serving on the International Students Committee, representing Southeast Asia. I was blessed by the monthly fellowship and pot-luck dinners, the International Day Celebration in the seminary chapel, the clothing closet, and many other facilities provided by international ministries.

Yet another special experience that serves as an example of the importance of international student ministries was my former church, University Baptist Church in Fort Worth, Texas. This is especially a good example of how the local church can become involved in ministry to international students, as we have been discussing. The church hosted international students at special events throughout the year. They also designated a house for international students with a host couple that lived there. Many international students were blessed by staying there for short periods of time. My family and I were blessed to stay there during a period of transit when we were moving into seminary housing, as well as during a short visit we made to the United States while I was serving in India. This ministry was open to all the international students, irrespective of their religion or ethnicity. These ministries provided a rich experience of meeting many other international students, and opened the door so we could share the love of Christ with them.

Conclusion

Christian Breuninger states that:

Effective church leaders must, in cooperation with the Holy Spirit and the body of Christ, learn how to become culture-creators, shaping communities that serve God's mission purposes by embedding a culture of mission in the church. (Breuninger, 21)

God's mission will be accomplished when all cultures have become citizens of God's Kingdom. To make this happen, pastors and other church leaders need to be open to the leadership of the Holy Spirit, and be sensitive to the needs of the community where they serve. If one wants to be effective in ministering cross-culturally, he needs to know his own culture first, and be willing to learn and appreciate other cultures as well. Mutual respect and crossing over to other cultures will allow the leader to expand the territory of his influence and do effective ministry. Proper implementation of cross-cultural ministry will enable the church to see a significant difference in its approach to ministry and, thus to grow in an ever increasingly multicultural society.

We must acknowledge that no matter what our culture, there are biblical emphases for leaders that are binding. Hebrews 13:17 tells us to "Obey your leaders and submit to their authority." However, Peter cautions leaders not to be guilty of "lording it over those entrusted to you"(1 Peter 5:3), but rather to be "examples to the flock" (1 Peter 5:3). Peter also calls leaders to "Be shepherds of God's flock that is under your care, serving as overseers—not because you must, but because you are willing" (1 Peter 5:2). The authority that leaders have is loaned to them by the Lord, and they are responsible directly to Him for the way they utilize it. The power is not to be imposed on others; it is rather given by God through the Holy Spirit to leaders and all Christians who avail themselves of God's gift in Christ, so they can carry out His ministry. While all relationships in life involve power, under the guidance of the Holy Spirit, one can learn how to use it for the good of others. The desire for excellence, while noble, should not be a cover for the seductive powers of greed and prestige. Creative use of power produces unity among people of all cultures. This is absolutely essential for those who would do cross-cultural ministry and lead a multicultural church (Roembke).

CONCLUSION

We have made the point in this book that the world is coming to America. Therefore, the church must be active in reaching out to the people of the various cultures that God is bringing to us. Carl Selle makes the point that reaching out cross-culturally is being a good steward of the opportunity and resources God has given the church. He writes:

> Christian denominations spend large sums each year to transport their workers outside of the States: internationals…come at no expense to the Christian church. A missionary spends many hours learning to communicate fluently in a second language: most internationals…speak English fluently. Mission boards know that forty countries are closed to traditional missionaries: many international students come from those very countries and are easily contacted while they study here. Missionaries often discover terrific resistance to Christianity because of family,

friends, surroundings, and culture: internationals...daily experience many new things
and are open to change. Missionaries confirm
that it is hard to be accepted by people in
closely knit communities who have friends,
customs, and culture in common: internationals...have left behind all that makes life
secure and are open to new relationships and
ideas. Missionaries find it useful if authorities
are favorably disposed toward them: as they
return home, international students may be
setting the guidelines for missionary activity
in their countries. (Selle, 23)

Selle's words should convict us that if we do not reach
out cross-culturally, we will miss a clear calling from
God that He has placed upon His church by placing
persons from around the world at our doorstep.

This calling to reach out to all persons is found
in Scripture. That is where we started this book
– focusing on the teachings of God's Word on the
topic. He confirms the call and opens the door for
us to fulfill that calling by bringing these folks to
us, as we also have demonstrated in this book. It is
our prayer that these facts will motivate you to get
involved in recognizing and following God's call.

Once you heed the call, you will need the tools
to carry out cross-cultural ministry. God does not
call us without providing what we need to fulfill it.
Therefore, we have also provided you with the tools
you need to do cross-cultural ministry. Again, these
have been gleaned from God's Word.

It is our prayer that you will teach these truths and tools to your church, and then lead them to put them into practice. Begin with key leaders in the church and let them spread the message with enthusiasm over what God does in their lives through that training. To help you do this, we have included as appendixes three things: (1) suggestions for teaching the material over a six week period; (2) a teaching plan for introducing the material in a weekend retreat setting; (3) some worksheets to be used while teaching the materials, whether in the weekly or weekend format. We likewise pray that the result of your use of the material in this book will be your church successfully reaching out to *all* persons in your community, and God's Kingdom being expanded for His glory. Rebecca Barnes writes: "Congregations are now discovering that in order to be churches of their community, for their community, they must learn to be a church of mirrors, reflecting their surrounding neighborhoods" (Barnes, 1). We pray that the material in this book will help your church be that mirror in your community.

APPENDIX 1

WEEKLY TRAINING PLAN

The following are suggestions for teaching the class in six weekly one hour sessions. You will need to have a copy of the book for each person to hand out at the first session. It is also assumed that the class leader has studied the church's community and has information about its ethnic/racial makeup.

Week 1

1. Begin by giving a brief devotional in which you explain using Scripture about your vision for reaching the community.

2. Give an overview of the community in which the church ministers based on research you have already done yourself, pointing out the differing types of persons living there that the church must reach.

3. Ask the church members present to discuss ways they can reach the community.

4. Hand out the book and discuss what you will be studying over the next few weeks.

5. Give class members their homework assignment: Read Chapter 1 in the book.

6. Pray that God will speak to each of you about reaching your community as you read the chapter during the week.

Week 2

1. After a welcome and opening prayer, divide the class members into groups of three to four persons each, and give each group a copy of the questions found in Appendix 3 that are based on Chapter 1 in the book. Allow the groups about twenty minutes to discuss the questions and then call them back into a large group.

2. Lead a discussion of the material in Chapter 1 of the book, using the questions as a starting point for each major section of the chapter.

3. Use the last question to discuss the need to commit to reach *all* persons in the church's community.

4. Give class members their homework assignment for next week: Read Chapter 2 in the book and be aware of people they observe in the community.

5. Close by praying that God will give your church a heart to reach *everyone* in the community the church serves, and that He will speak through their reading this week.

Week 3

1. After an opening prayer, divide the class members into groups of three to four persons each, and give each group a copy of the questions found in Appendix 4 that are based on Chapter 2 in the book. Allow the groups about twenty minutes to discuss the questions and then call them back into a large group.

2. Lead a discussion of the material in Chapter 2 of the book, using the questions as a starting point for each major section of the chapter. Make certain that you focus on the concept of ethnocentrism and how it hurts efforts to reach *everyone* in a community.

3. Ask for volunteers to tell what they observed about the church's community over the past week. Use question 5 to discuss the importance of being willing to change both as individuals and in terms of church structures, methodology, etc.

4. Give class members their homework assignment for next week: Read Chapter 3 in the book and continue to be aware of people they observe in the community.

5. Close with a prayer for God to make them open to change, to needs in the community, and to what God wants to teach them through Chapter 3 of the book.

Week 4

1. After an opening prayer, hand out copies of the "Understanding Other Cultures Worksheet," as found in Appendix 5. Give class members about ten minutes to write down their responses. Using the "Discussion Guide" found in Appendix 6, discuss each statement, how it helps us understand ways that cultures can be different, and how difficult it can be to minister across cultures because of these differences.

2. Using the material in Chapter 3, lead the class in a discussion of the importance of understanding who the people are that live in the community. Discuss ways that this understanding can be gained.

3. Lead the class in brainstorming some ways that they can learn more about the church's community and the people that live there. Try to get them to be specific.

4. Give class members their homework assignment for next week: Read Chapter 4 in the book and try to use one of the ideas discussed in the class time to get to know the church's community better. Tell them to wear shoes that are comfortable for walking next week.

5. Close with prayer, asking God to speak to each of you though the reading for the week, and through the activity you will do to understand your community better. Pray for insights into the needs of people in the community.

Week 5

1. After an opening prayer, divide the class into groups of three or four people each. Make certain there are men on each team. Give them a copy of "Researching Our Community" found in Appendix 7 attached to a clipboard with a pen or pencil. Explain that they will be assigned a section of the community to walk through while making observations, and the sheet they are being given will help them do that. Provide each team with a map of the community with a small area marked off that would be within reasonable walking distance of the community. Try to give each team an area that includes housing and at least a business or two. Pray for the teams and then send them out, asking them to return in thirty minutes.

2. When the teams return, lead in a debriefing time in which they discuss what they observed. Write what they relate about the community on large sheets of paper. Tell them to think about what is written on the sheets of paper during the week and try to determine what these things tell them about the community and how the church can best reach out to it. Tell them you will use this material next week in the final session.

3. Give class members their homework assignment for next week: Think about what they learned from today's session as described above. Hand out a copy of the "Community Member Questionnaire" found in Appendix 8 to each class member. Ask each class member to talk to one person who lives and/or works in the community, using the questionnaire as a guideline for the discussion.

4. Close with a prayer that God would use the things learned about the community this week to lead them to be more committed to reach the community with the Gospel, and that He might give them wisdom to know better how to do so.

Week 6

1. Before class, hang the sheets of paper with the observations from last week's community walk written on them. Have demographic

data about the community ready to hand out to class members.

2. After an opening prayer, ask members what they learned from talking to community members this past week. Add these observations to those already on the sheets of paper.

3. Ask class members what they learned from Chapter 4 in the book that might help them address some of the things they have identified in their study of the community thus far. Be prepared to point out topics you feel need to be addressed if they are not brought up by class members.

4. Divide the class into small groups of three to four members each. Give a copy of the demographic material about the community to each group. Ask each group to brainstorm about some specific steps the church could take to respond to the observations made about the community. Call the groups back together into a large group after about fifteen minutes. Have each group share their ideas and write them on another large sheet of paper. Have the class as a whole discuss which ideas they think would be good ones to begin working on soon, and which might make good long term goals for the church.

5. Ask class members to pray about becoming part of a team that would work to implement these ideas and others like them that you would develop after further study.

6. Thank the group for their participation in the class.

7. Close with a prayer that they might be open to God's leading in this area, and for the entire church to catch the vision of and to become involved in the process of reaching *all* persons in the church's community.

RETREAT PLAN

This plan is for a Friday night, Saturday retreat-type setting. It can be done at the church without an overnight stay, or at a retreat setting with an overnight stay. You will need to provide a copy of the book for everyone who is going to participate in the retreat ahead of time so they can read it before the retreat begins.

Friday Evening
7-8:00 P.M. Opening Session
1. Begin by giving a brief devotional in which you explain using Scripture about your vision for reaching the community.
2. Give an overview of the community in which the church ministers based on research you have already done yourself, pointing out the differing types of persons living there that the church must reach.

3. Ask the church members present to discuss ways they can reach the community.

4. Pray that God will speak to each of you about reaching your community during the weekend.

8-8:15 P.M. Break

8:15-9:15 P.M. Session 2

1. Divide the retreat members into groups of three to four persons each, and give each group a copy of the questions found in Appendix 3 that are based on Chapter 1 in the book. Allow the groups about twenty minutes to discuss the questions and then call them back into a large group.

2. Lead a discussion of the material in Chapter 1 of the book, using the questions as a starting point for each major section of the chapter.

3. Use the last question to discuss the need to commit to reach *all* persons in the church's community.

4. Close the evening by praying that God will give your church a heart to reach *everyone* in the community the church serves

Saturday Morning
9-10:00 A.M. Session 3

1. After an opening prayer, divide the retreat members into groups of three to four persons each, and give each group a copy of the questions in Appendix 4 that are based on Chapter

2 in the book. Allow the groups about twenty minutes to discuss the questions and then call them back into a large group.

2. Lead a discussion of the material in Chapter 2 of the book, using the questions as a starting point for each major section of the chapter. Make certain that you focus on the concept of ethnocentrism and how it hurts efforts to reach *everyone* in a community.

3. Use question 5 to discuss the importance of being willing to change both as individuals and in terms of church structures, methodology, etc.

4. Close the session with a prayer for God to make them open to change and to needs in the community.

10-10:15 A.M. **Break**

10:15-11:15 A.M. **Session 4**

1. After an opening prayer, hand out copies of the "Understanding Other Cultures Worksheet," as found in Appendix 5. Give retreat members about ten minutes to write down their responses. Using the "Discussion Guide" found in Appendix 6, discuss each statement, how it helps us understand ways that cultures can be different, and how difficult it can be to minister across cultures because of these differences.

2. Using the material in Chapter 3, lead the retreat members in a discussion of the importance of understanding who the people are that live in the community. Discuss ways that this understanding can be gained.

3. Lead the retreat members in brainstorming some ways that they can learn more about the church's community and the people who live there. Try to get them to be specific.

11:15 A.M.–11:30 P.M. Break

11:30 A.M.–12:30 P.M. Session 5

1. Have demographic and other data about the community that you have researched ahead of time ready to hand out to retreat members.

2. After an opening prayer, ask retreat members what they learned from Chapter 4 in the book that might help them address some of the things they have identified in their study of the community thus far. Be prepared to point out topics you feel need to be addressed if they are not brought up by retreat members.

3. Divide the retreat members into small groups of three to four members each. Give a copy of the demographic and other material about the community you have compiled to each group. Ask each group to brainstorm about what they can learn from the data and some specific steps the church could take to respond to the observations made about the commu-

nity. Ask them to write these down and be ready to share them with the whole group after lunch.

4. Close with prayer, asking God to speak to each of you though discussions around the lunch tables and through the afternoon session.

12:30 A.M.–1:30 P.M. **Lunch**

Saturday Afternoon
1:30-2:30 P.M. **Final Session**

1. After an opening prayer, have each group share the ideas they wrote down about ways the church could respond to the community, and write them on a large sheet of paper so all can see them. Have the group as a whole discuss which ideas they think would be good ones to begin working on soon, and which might make good long term goals for the church.

2. Ask retreat members to pray about becoming part of a team that would work to implement these ideas and others like them that you would develop after further study.

3. Thank the group for their participation in the retreat.

4. Close the retreat with a time of prayer. Ask retreat participants to share what God has taught them during the weekend. Then pray together, asking God for guidance and wisdom as you take new steps together.

APPENDIX 3

CROSS-CULTURAL/ MULTICULTURAL MINISTRY WORKSHEET

Answer the following questions based on information in the book, *Cross-Cultural Leadership: Ministering in a Multicultural Community*. Record your responses and be ready to share them with the rest of the group.

1. What is a multicultural church?

2. Why are multicultural churches needed?

3. How does what is taking place in our community compare to what is happening around the country?

4. What does God teach in His Word about ministering to other cultures?

5. What does this say to us about ministering to the people in our community?

APPENDIX 4

FOUNDATIONAL TRUTHS FOR MULTICULTURAL MINISTRY WORKSHEET

R ead carefully and answer each of the following questions based on Chapter 2 of the book, *Cross-Cultural Leadership: Ministering in a Multicultural Community*. Record your responses and be ready to discuss them with the larger group.

1. Which of the foundational truths explained in the chapter do you think is most important? Why?

2. Which do you think is the most difficult to apply in your life and church? Why?

3. Which stage for developing cultural sensitivity by individuals presented in the chapter do you think you are at?

4. Which stage for developing the ability to reach out cross-culturally by organizations presented in the chapter do you think our church is at?

5. What changes do you need to make to be more culturally sensitive? What changes does our church need to make?

UNDERSTANDING OTHER CULTURES WORKSHEET

Read each of the following statements and write how you would interpret each. Be ready to share your responses with the rest of the group.

1. A person comes to your appointment thirty minutes late.

2. A male guest helps a hostess carry dirty dishes from the table to the kitchen.

3. A man puts his arm around his own wife in your presence.

4. You see a woman jog by your house by herself early in the morning.

5. Someone asks you several personal questions as you begin a meeting, i.e., how is your family doing, how has your day been, etc.?

6. A person stands close to you and looks you in the eye as he talks to you.

7. You make a statement of fact and another person corrects you.

APPENDIX 6

DISCUSSION GUIDE FOR UNDERSTANDING OTHER CULTURES WORKSHEET

Read each of the following statements and write how you would interpret each:

1. A person comes to your appointment thirty minutes late.

    Explain that how people view time is one of the most important aspects of culture.

    Use the information from Chapter 3 on "Time" for more information to discuss on this topic.

    Explain that to a time oriented culture like most Americans follow, this would be very irritating. To an event oriented culture, it would not be a major problem.

2. A male guest helps a hostess carry dirty dishes from the table to the kitchen.

   Explain that in American culture, this would be normal.

   In some other cultures, it would be unacceptable.

3. A man puts his arm around his own wife in your presence.

   Explain that in American culture this is done all the time.

   Many cultures consider this an inappropriate gesture of public affection.

4. You see a woman jog by your house by herself early in the morning.

   Explain that this would be a common sight in the United States.

   In other cultures, a woman jogging might be seen as being in distress.

5. Someone asks you several personal questions as you begin a meeting, i.e., how is your family doing, how has your day been, etc.?

   Explain that this could be viewed in many different ways.

   Some cultures might view such personal talk as poor use of time in a meeting setting.

   Other cultures might view it as a necessity before business can begin.

6. A person stands close to you and looks you in the eye as he talks to you.

   Explain that how closely we stand to people while we talk to them is called personal space. This and things like whether or not we touch the other person as we talk differ greatly among various cultures.

   Americans do not like to stand too close or to do a lot of touching.

   Other cultures like to stand much closer and do a lot of touching.

   See the discussion of "Communication Style" in Chapter 3 for more on this.

7. You make a statement of fact and another person corrects you.

   Explain that this would be common in the United States.

   In some other cultures, it would be considered rude.

   See the discussion of "Communication Style" in Chapter 3 for more on this.

APPENDIX 7

RESEARCHING OUR COMMUNITY

Today you are going to put into practice one aspect of researching a community. Each team will be asked to walk through a specified community. You will record your observations about the community in the space below. Some areas for you to look for have been suggested.

1. What types of people do you see racially/ ethnically?

2. What types of people do you see socio-economically?

3. What types of troubled people do you see? (Homeless, neglected, gang members, etc.)

4. What age categories do you see or what evidence of age categories (bikes, toys, etc.) do you see and approximately in what percentage?

5. What type (single family, apartments, etc.) and condition of housing do you see?

6. What community resources do you see (churches, schools, parks, etc.)?

7. Visit a grocery store or other business in the community. What types of food and other items does the grocery store carry? What other unique aspects of businesses do you see that might help you understand more about the community?

8. What other observations can you make about the community that can help us understand it better?

APPENDIX 8

COMMUNITY MEMBER QUESTIONNAIRE

INTRODUCTION: "Hi, my name is _____. I'm from (*church's name*) and I'm asking some questions to find out more about our community. I'd appreciate a few minutes of your time to help me with this.

1. How long have you lived in this neighborhood?

2. Do you like it here?

3. What one or two things do you like most about it?

4. What one or two things do you like least about it?

5. What changes have you seen in the community in the time you have lived here?

6. What are the greatest needs you would identify in our community?

7. What church do you attend?

8. Is your church addressing any of these needs?

BIBLIOGRAPHY

Addison, Elaine. "Culture Shock: A Fish Out of Water" [on-line]. Accessed 27 June 2006. Available from http://www.johnesl.com/templates/reading/cultureshock/; Internet.

Anderson, Leith. *Dying for Change*. Minneapolis, MN: Bethany House, 1990.

Augsburger, David W. *Pastoral Counseling Across Cultures*. Philadelphia: Westminster Press, 1986.

Barnes, Albert. *Acts*. Barnes' Notes on the Old & New Testaments. Grand Rapids, MI: Baker Book House, 1977.

_____. *Isaiah*. Barnes' Notes on the Old and New Testament. Grand Rapids, MI: Baker Book House, 1977.

Barclay, William. *Letters to the Corinthians*. The Daily Study Bible. Philadelphia: The Westminster Press, 1956.

_____. *The Acts of the Apostles*. The Daily Study Bible. Philadelphia: The Westminster Press, 1955.

_____. *The Gospel of John*. The Daily Study Bible. Philadelphia: The Westminster Press, 1956.

Barna, George. *The Power of Vision*. Wheaton, IL: Scripture Press, 1977.

Barnes, Rebecca. "Church of Mirrors." *Outreach* (May/June 2005).

Beasley-Murray, George R. *John*. Word Biblical Commentary, vol. 36. Waco, TX: Word Books, 1987.

Beckhard, Richard and Wendy Pritchard. *Changing the Essence: The Art of Creating and Leading Fundamental Change in Organizations*. San Francisco: Jossey-Bass, 1992.

Belgum, David. "Dealing with Cultural Diversity: A Hospital Chaplain Reflects on Gypsies and Other Such Diversity." *The Journal of Pastoral Care* 53 (Summer 1999).

Bennis, Warren and Burt Nanus. *Leaders: The Strategies for Taking Charge*. New York: Harper & Row, 1985.

Blommaert, Jan. "Ideologies in Intercultural Communication." In *Intercultural Communication And Contact: Selected Papers Presented at the Nordic Symposium at the Centre for Inercucltural Communication, School of Mission and Theology*, 24-26 November 1994, edited by Oyvind Dahl. Misjonshogskolen forlog, Stavanger: Trykkeriet Impress AS.

Boice, James Montgomery. *Galatians*. In vol. 10 of *The Expositor's Bible Commentary*. Edited by Frank E. Gaebelein. Grand Rapids, MI: Zondervan, 1976.

Borchert, Gerald L. *John 1-11*. The New American Commentary, vol. 25A. Nashville, TN: Broadman and Holman, 1996.

_____. *John 12-21*. The New American Commentary, vol. 25B. Nashville, TN: Broadman and Holman, 2002.

Breneman, Mervin. *Ezra, Nehemiah, Esther*. The New American Commentary, vol. 10. Nashville, TN: Broadman & Holman, 1993.

Breuninger, Christian B. "Creating a Culture of Mission in the Church." *Covenant Quarterly* 56 (May 1998).

Brewster, E. Thomas and Elizabeth S. Brewster. "To Communicate Effectively." Lecture at the Agape International Training (Arrowhead Springs, CA, 1974).

Bruce, F.F. *Commentary on the Book of Acts*. The New International Commentary on the New Testament. Grand Rapids, MI: Wm. B. Eerdman's, 1979.

Burdick, Donald W. *James*. In vol. 12 of *The Expositor's Bible Commentary*. Edited by Frank E. Gaebelein, 159-205. Grand Rapids, MI: Zondervan, 1981.

Carson, D. A. *Matthew*. In vol. 8 of *The Expositor's Bible Commentary*. Edited by Frank E. Gaebelein, 1-599. Grand Rapids, MI: Zondervan, 1984.

Canales, Isaac and Erin Dufault. *Multi-Ethnicity*. Downers Grove, IL: InterVarsity Press, 1990.

Clasper, Paul. *Eastern Paths and the Christian Way*. Maryknoll, NY: Orbis Books, 1982.

Clement, Atchenemou Hlama, Raymond Hassan, Moyo Ozodo, and Bill Kornfield. *Cross-Cultural Christianity: A Text Book on Cross-Cultural Communication*. Jos, Nigeria:

Nigeria Evangelical Missionary Institute, 1996.

Cole, R. A. *The Epistle of Paul to the Galatians.* The Tyndale New Testament Commentaries. Grand Rapids, MI: Wm. B. Eerdmans, 1978.

DeGenova, Mary Kay. *Families in Cultural Context.* Mountain View, CA: Mayfield Publishing, 1997.

Delaney, Joan. "My Pilgrimage in Mission." *International Bulletin of Missionary Research* 25 (January 2001).

Dunne, John. *The Way of All the Earth: Experiments in Truth and Religion.* New York: Macmillan, 1972.

Easterley, William. "Empirics of Strategic Interdependence: The Case of the Racial Tipping Point" [on-line]. Accessed 4 July 2006. Available from http://emlab.berkeley.edu/users/webfac/emiguel/e271_s04/easterly.pdf; Internet.

Ellen, Ingrid Gould. "Race-Based Neighborhood Projection: A Proposed Framework for Understanding New Data on Racial Integration [on-line]. Accessed 4 July 2006. Available from http://urban.nyu.edu/research/integration/index.htm; Internet.

Elmer, Duane. *Cross Cultural Conflict: Building Relationships for Effective Ministry*. Downers Grove, IL: InterVarsity Press, 1993.

Ford, Leighton. *The Christian Persuader*. New York: Harper & Row, 1966.

Fergusson, David. "The Doctrine of the Incarnation Today." *Expository Times* 113 (December, 2001).

Fredrickson, Roger L. *John*. The Communicator's Commentary, vol. 4. Waco, TX: Word Books, 1983.

Gargner, John. "The Tasks of Leadership, Leadership. *Leadership Papers 2*. Washington, DC: Leadership Studies Program, Independent Sector, 1986.

George, Timothy. *Galatians*. The New American Commentary, vol. 30. Nashville: Broadman & Holman, 1994.

Goette, Robert D. "Srating a Multicultural Church" [on-line]. Accessed 19 July 2006. Available from http://www.mbcb. org/download/cp/Starting%20a%20Multi-Cultural%20Church.pps; Internet.

Goetz, David L. "The Riddle of Our Postmodern Culture: What Is Postmodernism? Should We Even Care?" *Leadership* 18 (Winter 1997).

"Golden Gate Seminary Receives Major Gift for School of Intercultural Studies." *GGBTS News* (December 1995).

Greenleaf, Robert K. *Servant Leadership*. New York: Paulist Press, 1977.

Grogan, Geoffrey W. *Isaiah*. In vol. 6 of *The Expositor's Bible Commentary*. Edited by Frank E. Gaebelein, 1-354. Grand Rapids, MI: Zondervan, 1986.

Grunlan, Stephan A. and Marvin K. Mayers. *Cultural Anthropology: A Christian Perspective*. Grand Rapids, MI: Zondervan, 1979.

Guffey, Betty R. *Bring the World to Your Home*. Colorado Springs, CO: International Students, Inc. n.d.

Hall, Edward T. *Beyond Culture*. Garden City, NJ: Doubleday Anchor Press, 1976.

Hebblewait, Brian. "The Impossibility of Multiple Incarnations." *Theology* 104 (September-October, 2001).

Henry, Matthew. *Luke 17 to John 8*. Mathew Henry's Commentary on the New Testament, vol. 4. Grand Rapids, MI: Baker Book House, 1983.

Hesselgrave, David J. *Planting Churches Cross-Culturally: North America and Beyond*, 2nd ed. Grand Rapids, MI: Baker Books, 2000.

Hesselgrave, David J. and Edward Rommen. *Contextualization: Meaning, Methods, and Models*. Pasadena, CA: William Carey Library, 2000.

Hiebert, Paul G. *Anthropological Insights for Missionaries*. Grand Rapids, MI: Baker Book House, 1985.

His Heart Our Hands. Alpharetta, GA: North American Mission Board of the Southern Baptist Convention, 2000.

Hobbs, Herschel H. "Biblical Concepts Of Equality." In *The Nation Of Prejudice*. Edited by John A. Ishee. Nashville, Tennessee: The Sunday School Board of the Southern Baptist Convention, 1969.

Hunke, Dixie L. *Attitudes and Etiquette: Ministering Cross-Culturally*. Birmingham, AL: New Hope, 1989.

Johnson, Sherman E. *Matthew & Mark*. The Interpreter's Bible, vol. 7. New York: Abington Press, 1952.

Jordan, John E. "An Outline of Some Aspects, Concerns, Dimensions, and Areas of Activity to Be Considered in an International Campus Community." Outline prepared on the basis of discussion and recommendations at the CCWAIS-NSCF Consultation on Developing Ecumenical Ministry among the International Community on U.S. Campuses (Chicago, IL, 3-5 January 1965).

Keil, C. F. and F. Delitzsch. *Isaiah*. Commentary on the Old Testament, vol. VII. Translated by James Martin. Grand Rapids, MI: Wm. B. Eerdmans, 1978.

Kraft, Charles H. *Culture, Communication and Christianity: A Selection of Writings by Charles H. Kraft*. Pasadena, CA: William Carey Library, 2001.

Lane, Patty. *A Beginner's Guide to Crossing Cultures*. Downers Grove, IL: InterVarsity Press, 2002.

Lau, Lawson. *The World at Your Door Step: A Handbook for International Student Ministry*. Downers Grove, IL: InterVarsity Press, 1984.

Law, Eric H. F. "Lessons for Diversity from the Spiritual Realm." In *Cultural Diversity Sourcebook*. Edited by Bob Abrammms and George F. Simons. Boston, MA: HRD Press, 1996.

Lawson, Linda. "Churches Enriched by Diversity." *Facts and Trends*. (March 1996).

Lingenfelter, Sherwood. *Transforming Culture: A Challenge for Christian Mission.* Grand Rapids, MI: Baker Book House, 1992.

Lingenfelter, Sherwood G. and Marvin K. Mayers. *Ministering Cross-Culturally: An Incarnational Model for Personal Relationships.* 2nd ed. Grand Rapids, MI: Baker Book House, 2003.

Little, Paul E. *A Guide to International Friendship*. Madison,WI.: InterVarsity Christian Fellowship, 1959.

Longenecker, Richard N. *Galatians*. Word Biblical Commentary, vol. 4. Dallas, Texas: Word Books, 1990.

_____. *The Acts of the Apostles*. In vol. 9 of *The Expositior's Bible Commentary*. Edited by Frank E. Gaebelein, 205-573. Grand Rapids, MI: Zondervan, 1981.

Lyons, Charles. "Living Color." *Leadership* 20 (Fall 1999).

Madsen, William. *The Mexican Americans of South Texas.* New York: Holt, Rinehart, and Winston, 1964.

Malphurs, Aubrey. *Ministry Nuts and Bolts: What They Don't Teach Pastors in Seminary.* Grand Rapids, MI: Kregel, 1997.

Massie, Milton and Marc Hinkel. "Promoting Racial Reconciliation in the City." In *A Heart for the City.* Edited by John Fuder. Chicago: Moody Press, 1999.

Matthews, Kenneth A. *Genesis 11:27 - 50:26.* The New American Commentary, vol. 1B. Nashville, TN: Broadman & Holman, 2005.

Maudlin, Michael G. "God's Contractor: How Habitat for Humanity's Millard Fuller Persuaded Corporate America to Do Kingdom Work." *Christianity Today* 43 (14 June 1999).

Mayers, Marvin K. *Christianity Confronts Culture: A Strategy for Cross-Cultural Evangelism.* Grand Rapids, MI: Zondervan, 1987.

McConnell, William T. *The Gift of Time.* Downers Grove, IL: InterVarsity, 1983.

Mare, W. Harold. *1 Corinthians*. In vol. 10 of *The Expositor's Bible Commentary*. Edited by Frank E. Gaebelein, 173-297. Grand Rapids, MI: Zondervan, 1976.

Melick, Richard R., Jr. *Philippians, Colossians, Philemon*. The New America Commentary. Nashville, TN: Broadman Press, 1991.

Mhlophe, Fanyana P. "The Effects of Apartheid on Baptist Convention Pastors in South Africa." In *TheBarkley West National Awareness Workshop*. Edited by Des Hoffmeister and Brian J. Gurney. Johannesburg, South Africa: The Awareness Campaign of the Baptist Convention of South Africa, 1990.

Moreau, Scott. "The Messy Tension Between Syncretism and Contextualization," *Mission Maker Magazine* (2006).

Niebuhr, Richard, H. *Christ and Culture*. New York: Harper and Row, Harper Torch Books, 1956.

O'Brien, Peter T. *Colossians, Philemon*. Word Biblical Commentary, vol. 44. Waco, TX: Word, 1982.

Ortiz, Manuel. *One New People: Models for Developing a Multiethnic Church*. Downers Grove, IL: InterVarsity Press, 1996.

Phan, Peter C. "Doing Theology in the Context of Mission: Lessons from Alexandre de Rhodes, S.J." *Gregorianum* 81 (April 2000).

Pocock, Michael and Joseph Henriques. *Cultural Change and Your Church: Helping Your Church Thrive in a Diverse Society.* Grand Rapids, MI: Baker, 2002.

Polhill John B. *Acts.* The New American Commentary, vol. 26. Nashville: Broadman Press, 1992.

Popenoe, David. *Sociology*, 11th ed. Upper Saddle River, NJ: Prentice Hall, 2000.

Qadeer, Mohammed. "Ethnic Segregation in a Multicultural City." *Ceris Working Paper Series*, no. 28. Toronto, Canada: Joint Centre of Excellence for Research on Immigration and Settlement (October 2003).

Queen, Stuart A., Robert W. Habenstein, and Jill S. Quadagno. *The Family in Various Cultures.* New York: Harper and Row, 1985.

Rennstich, Karl. "Missionarische Ethik" (Unpublished 1996).

Rhodes, Stephen A. *Where Nations Meet: The Church in a Multicultural World.* Downers Grove, IL: InterVarsity Press, 1998.

Richardson, Kurt A. *James*. The New American Commentary, vol. 36. Nashville, TN: Broadman & Holman, 1997.

Roembke, Lianne. *Building Credible Multicultural Teams*. Pasadena, CA: William Carey Library, 2000.

Romo, Oscar I. *Missions in Ethnic America*. Atlanta, GA: HMB SBC, 1988.

Rottenberg, Isaac C. "The Body of Christ and the Embodiment of Christianity." *Perspectives* 16 (May 2001).

Ruffle, Douglas W. "Building Blocks for a Multicultural Congregation." *Quarterly Review* 13 (Fall 1993).

Ryan, Skip. "How Jesus Transforms the Church" *Journal of Biblical Counseling* 17. (Winter, 1999).

Salins, Peter D. *Assimilation, American Style: An Impassioned Defense of Immigration and Assimilation as the Foundation of American Greatness and the American Dream*. New York: Basic Books, 1997.

Schaller, Lyle A. *New Results: New Ideas in Church Vitality and Leadership*. 10 (March 1989).

Schein, Edgar H. *Organizational Culture and Leadership*, 2nd ed. San Francisco: Jossey-Bass, 1997.

Seilhamer, Ray A. "Leadership: A Counter-Culture Perspective" *Evangelical Journal* 11 (Fall 1993).

Selle, Carl. "A Ministry of Friendship to Those at Our Doorstep." *Missio Apostolic* 6 (May 1998).

Shorter, Aylward. *Evangelization and Culture*. London: Geoffrey Chapman, 1994.

Simpson, E. K. and F.F. Bruce. *The Epistles to the Ephesians and the Colossians*. The New International Commentary on the New Testament. Grand Rapids, MI: Wm. B. Eerdmans, 1979.

Smith, Donald K. *Creating Understanding*. Grand Rapids, MI: Zondervan, 1992.

Stafford, Jim. "Here Comes the World." *Christianity Today* 39 (15 May 1995).

Stein, Robert H. *Luke*. The New American Commentary, vol. 24. Nashville, TN: Broadman Press, 1992.

Stewart, Edward C. *American Cultural Patterns: A Cross-Cultural Perspective*. Yarmouth, ME: Intercultural Press, 1985.

Stott, John R.W. *Christian Mission in the Modern World*. Downers Grove, IL: InterVarsity Press, 1975.

_____. *The Message of Acts*. Downers Grove, IL: InterVarsity Press, 1990.

Tasker, R.V.G. *The Gospel According to John*. Tyndale New Testament Commentaries, vol. 4. Grand Rapids, MI: Wm. B. Eerdmans, 1973.

Taussig, Bob and Mary. *Helping International Students Oreintation Handbook*. Manhattan, KS: Helping International Students, 1982.

Tenney, Merrill C. *John*. In vol. 9 of *The Expositor's Bible Commentary*. Edited by Frank E. Gaebelein, 1-203. Grand Rapids, MI: Zondervan, 1981.

Thompson, J.A. *1, 2 Chronicles*. The New American Commentary, vol. 9. Nashville: Broadman & Holman, 1994.

Thurber, L. Newton. "Perspectives on Ecumenical Christian Presence in US Universities and

Colleges 1960-1995." *Journal of Ecumenical Studies* 32 (Fall 1995).

Wall, Robert W. *Colossians & Philemon*. The IVP New Testament Commentary Series. Downers Grove, IL: InterVarsity, 1993.

Weber, Charles W. "Mission Strategies, Anthropologists, and the Harmon Foundation's African Film Projects: Presenting Africa to the Public in the Inter-War Years" *Missiology* 29 (January 2001).

Willard, Dallas. "Taking God's Keys: The Keys of the Kingdom Also Unlock the Joys of Your Calling" *Leadership* 19 (Fall, 1998).

Willimon, William H. "Everyone Whom the Lord Our God Calls: Acts 2 and the Miracle of Pentecost Preaching in a Multicultural Context." *Journal for Preachers* 25 (Pentecost 2004).

Yancey, George. *One Body One Spirit*. Downers Grove, IL: InterVarsity Press, 2003.

Zodhiates, Spiros, comp. and ed. *The Complete Word Study Dictionary: New Testament*. Chattanooga, TN: AMG, 1992.

Printed in the United States
60526LVS00001B/124-204